THE WINE BOOK

A Guide to Choosing and Enjoying Wine

by
Rosalind Cooper

Produced by London Editions Limited, 70
Old Compton Street, London W1V 5PA
Editor: Janet Sacks
Design: Nigel Soper and Richard Dewing,
Millions Design
Art Director: Nigel Soper
Special Photos: Peter Myers

For H.P. Books
Publisher: Bill Fisher
Executive Editor: Carl Shipman
Editorial Director: Helen Fisher
Editor: Theodore DiSante
Art Director: Don Burton
Book Assembly: Dana Martin
Typography: Cindy Coatsworth,
Joanne Nociti, Michelle Claridge

Published by HP Books, P.O. Box 5367
Tucson, AZ 85703
(602) 888-2150
ISBN: 0-89586-131-3
Library of Congress Catalog Card Number:
81-83534
©1981 Fisher Publishing Inc.
Printed in USA

R. de Chadelles Champagne;
Chianti Antinori 1978;
Rhine Bear Liebfraumilch 1978;
Christian Brothers' Dry Sherry.

Contents

Introduction

People are becoming more and more interested in wine. This is due to the extensive selection of domestic and international wines. Such a huge variety, however, can be confusing when you want to choose a wine.

There are people who create a mystique about wine. They can give you the impression that if you don't know everything about the subject you can't enjoy it. This is not true! In the wine countries of Europe wine is an everyday drink enjoyed with meals and friends. The same is happening elsewhere in the world, as people learn more about wine and share their knowledge, and wine, with friends.

This book will help you make choices confidently. It provides a simple and clear guide to the wines of the world, so you can choose the kind of wine you prefer. France, Germany and Italy are traditionally considered the best wine producers, but many other nations rival their products in quality and price.

In Europe, Spain and Portugal are gaining reputations for high-quality wines. Even Iron-Curtain countries like Bulgaria, Romania and Hungary export good wines.

However, it is outside of Europe that the most exciting developments have occurred. California has a vigorous industry, backed by research into grape-growing and wine-making technology. Australia, with a climate similar to California's, also makes fine wine. South American and South African wines, too, are gaining acceptance in the world of wine.

After you choose your wine, you will want to know how and where to keep it. This is very simple, even if you don't have a cellar. You'll also learn about serving wine and which foods complement different types best. In addition you'll find information about appetizer and dessert wines. There are recipes for cold and hot wine-based drinks to serve at a party or enjoy on a hot summer day.

By reading this book, you'll learn all you need to know to enjoy choosing and drinking your next bottle of wine.

1

ENYOYING WINE

Luncheon of the Boating Party by Pierre
Auguste Renoir (1814-1919).
Phillips Collection, Washington D.C.

Some Basics

The very first wine was probably made by chance. One ancient Persian legend says that a grape-loving king stored ripe grapes in a cellar so he could enjoy grapes all year long. Some bruised grapes began fermenting, giving off carbon dioxide gas that temporarily knocked out some slaves in the cellar. One of the king's rejected, distraught mistresses decided to drink this poison potion, only to leave the cellar singing and dancing in high spirits. The king realized that his fruity liquid had the wonderful and mysterious power to make sad people happy. His discovery is something we share to this day.

Our earliest archaeological evidence of wine-making points to neolithic Persia. Writings about wine are dated from 3,000 B.C. By 1,500 B.C. there was a lively wine trade in Phoenecia, Lebanon, Syria, Egypt, Crete and other Middle Eastern nations. Gods, goddesses, legends and songs about wine and grapes were created by different cultures to celebrate the importance of wine.

In the Bible, vineyards are mentioned as valuable possessions because they give both food and drink. Wine is also the sacred beverage for many religions. Because of its alcoholic content, wine's medicinal qualities have been recognized throughout the ages.

Ancient Greeks are usually credited with introducing grape vines into Western Europe. However, the Romans distributed it much farther as their conquests grew. Roman legions occupying Germany, Spain, Portugal and England planted grape vines and made wine. This helped to boost morale and gave the troops something to do when not defending the empire.

During the centuries following the fall of the Roman Empire, monasteries continued to propagate vineyards and make wine. As the power of Christianity spread, so did the culture of wine. Grapes and wine-making knowledge accompanied missionaries and explorers to the New World. Today, wine is made and consumed all over the world.

WHAT IS WINE?

In simple terms, wine is the result of yeast feeding on the sugars of ripe grapes in the presence of air. Yeast is a living, cellular organism. It naturally occurs on ripe grapes as the thin, waxy coating called the *bloom*.

After the skin of the grape breaks, the multitude of tiny yeast cells on the skin begins reacting with the sugars in the juice, turning it to alcohol. In addition, the yeast cells also produce carbon dioxide gas. This makes the crushed grapes bubbly and frothy during the process. You can make wine from any fruit. But with fruits other than grapes you have to add sugar to help the yeast cells. Only grapes produce enough sugar for this reaction to occur naturally.

Yeast action on the grapes is called *fermentation*. If crushed grapes are left to ferment naturally, the yeast usually consumes all of the sugar available, giving it an alcoholic concentration from about 10 to 13%. This makes an unsweet wine described as *dry*.

Wine makers vary this basic process to create different kinds of wines. For example, if all of the carbon dioxide gas created during fermentation does not escape, the wine is fizzy. This is how sparkling wines and champagne are made.

If the sugar content of the grapes is very high, the yeast can't consume all of it before being poisoned by the high concentration of alcohol produced— about 15%. This makes a sweet wine with a high alcoholic content.

Temperature control is critical in fine wine-making. If the wine sours due to improper temperature control, vinegar results. If the residue of crushed grapes remains in the new wine, it affects the wine's flavor and appearance. Some grapes are fermented with skins, some aren't.

After fermentation, some wines are bottled, and others are stored and aged in wooden casks. It is not enough to let wine make itself—it needs some help from man to become its best.

Below: This is a detail from the 12th century B.C. tomb of Nakht at Thebes. Shown is grape gathering at the arbor.

Below, opposite page: Ripe grapes ready to become wine are cut from the vine.

      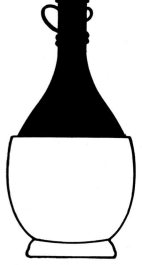

Sherry is usually sold in a heavy, broad-shouldered bottle with a long neck.

Red and white Burgundy come in green bottles with sloping shoulders.

A bottle of claret has a square shoulder and is made of green glass.

German wine bottles are tall; green for Mosel, brown for Rhine.

Champagne bottles are thick and sturdy to withstand pent-up pressure.

Loire Valley wines come in slimmer and paler bottles than Burgundies.

Chianti is available in a straw-covered flask, called *fiasco*.

How Wine is Made

To make the extensive variety of wines available, wine makers have developed special techniques for different grapes and regions. This makes the world of wine an exciting and never-ending source of pleasure.

RED WINES

Making red wine is easy to understand. Essentially, the colors and distinctive tastes of red wines are due to the skins of the grape fermenting with the grape juice. This mixture of skins, juice and seeds is called *must*.

Grape Picking and Crushing—The red grape varieties that become red wines are picked when the grower thinks they are fully ripe. They are quickly taken to the winery and put into a crushing machine. Speed is vital to ensure the ripe grapes are in prime condition and do not begin to ferment too early. Some winemakers remove the stalks from the grape bunches at this stage.

After grapes are crushed, they begin fermenting in a fermentation vat. It may be made of stainless steel, or wood or cement lined with glass or porcelain. Yeast cells that were on the grape skins go to work to convert the sugar to alcohol. The mixture begins to foam and froth as it ferments, liberating carbon dioxide gas. In some areas the native yeasts on the grapes do not give best results, so other specially prepared yeasts are added to the vat.

During fermentation the grape skins release color and *tannic acid*. This gives red wine an astringent taste also described as *harsh* or *tart*. Tannic acid is in all red wines. The wine maker controls the amount of tannic acid in the wine by controlling how long the grape skins ferment with the juice.

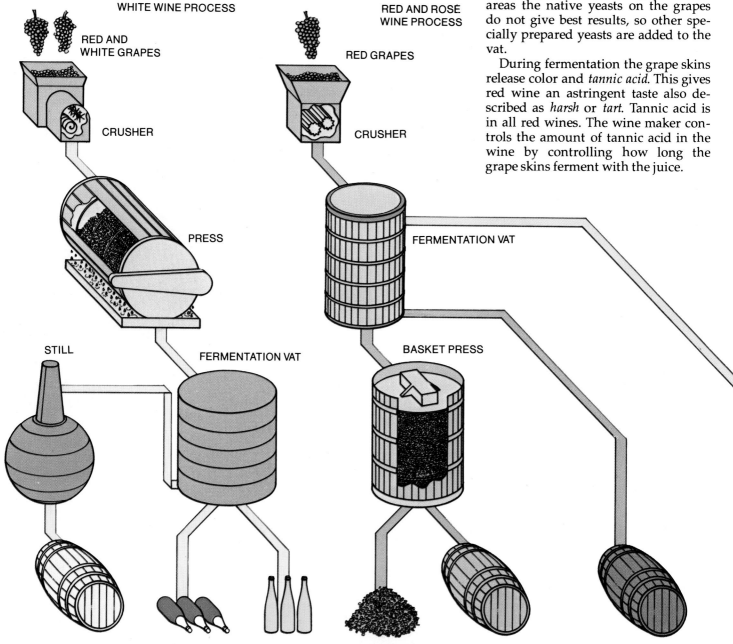

WHITE WINE PROCESS

RED AND WHITE GRAPES

CRUSHER

PRESS

STILL

FERMENTATION VAT

RED AND ROSÉ WINE PROCESS

RED GRAPES

CRUSHER

FERMENTATION VAT

BASKET PRESS

Brandy is made by distilling white wine or *marc*. It is aged in wooden casks.

Champagne is white wine bottled after its first fermentation. It ferments a second time in the bottle.

White wine is rarely aged in wood. Usually, it is bottled after fermentation to keep it tasting young and fresh.

Marc is distilled from the residue of skins, seeds and stalks after grapes are pressed.

Press wine is made by pressing residue skins that have already been pressed. It is a coarse wine.

Fine red wines are aged in wooden barrels after fermentation.

Cellaring—Wines that are to be consumed soon are *pressed* quickly before much tannic acid is released by the skins, stalks, and seeds. The must is squeezed to release fermented juices. The pressed wine continues fermenting in a secondary vat without the skins and stalks. This makes them drinkable without aging.

Fine wines are processed to have the most tannic acid. This promotes a dark, rich color. Proper aging mellows the wine and makes it most drinkable years later. Fine red wines are always stored in wooden casks that impart additional flavor to the wine and allow air to seep in and subtly alter it.

While the wines mature, they are usually *racked* one or more times. This is transferring the wine through a pipe to another cask. Because sediment is left behind with each transfer, the wine has a brighter appearance after each racking.

After aging in wood, the wine is bottled. It continues to age and improve in the bottle when properly stored.

WHITE WINES

White wine is made from either white or red grapes. Grape juice that becomes white wine is not fermented with skins.

Grape Picking and Pressing—Soon after being picked, the stalks of ripe grapes are removed. Then the grapes

These ripe grapes show natural yeasts, called *bloom*, on their skins.

are pressed. Stalks have some tannic acid and other bitter-tasting chemicals that are undesirable in delicate white wine. Under pressure, the grape juice runs out. The seeds remain unbroken. Like stalks, grape seeds can add bitterness to wine.

Fermentation—Juice runs from the press into a fermentation vat. For white wines, most modern wineries use a stainless steel vat because its temperature can be carefully controlled. The grapes ferment as described earlier.

Cellaring—Most white wines are at their best when young and fresh. The aim of the wine maker is to preserve this freshness by avoiding contact with air, which ages wine. This aging process is desirable with many red wines because it improves flavor. But with very few exceptions, this type of aging makes white wine dull and flat.

In the cellar, white wines are stored in cool conditions and filtered to remove any trace of sediment that could affect their attractive color. Some white wines are best when consumed *young*, within a few months after bottling. Most others are best when aged for a year or two under proper conditions.

PINK WINES

Pink, or *rosé*, wines are pale red wines. They are usually made by leaving the grape skins in contact with the

juice for a very short time, often less than a day. This gives just enough color to turn the wine pink, but not deep red. The brief contact with the skins also gives additional flavor. The wines are then processed in the same way as white wines.

An alternate method is to blend a little red wine with white until a desirable mixture is obtained. This method is not used for the finest rosé wines, but many very drinkable pink wines are made this way.

OTHER WINES

Like a good farmer, the wine maker knows how to make the most of what is produced. Nothing involved in the wine-making process goes to waste.

Press Wine—After fermentation and pressing, there is always a residue of skins left in the vat. In the case of white wine, the skins are not part of the fermentation process. Using the same press that 'squeezes' the juice for white wine, the wine maker can press all the residue of skins, seeds and stalks to make *press wine*. It ferments in the usual way, but is not of top quality. The stalks can give this wine a bitter flavor.

Brandy—Brandy is a distilled spirit like vodka, gin or whisky. The difference is that it is made from wine, not grain or potatoes. The name *brandy* is derived from an old Dutch word that literally means *burnt wine*, which gives a clue to the way it is made.

Brandy can be made from either low-quality white wine or the residue left after pressing the grapes. The wine or residue is heated in a specially designed container until it evaporates. The alcoholic vapor given off is collected and cooled. This process is called *distillation*. The condensed liquid is then redistilled to remove impurities. The result is a white spirit that goes into wooden casks.

After several years, the wood gives the white spirit a brown color and imparts a pungent flavor. Much of the young brandy evaporates through the porous wood, so the brandy must be replenished with extra spirit. This gradual evaporation concentrates the flavor of the brandy until the day it is transferred to bottles for shipment. In Cognac, the French region that produces fine brandy, the evaporated spirit is called "the angel's share."

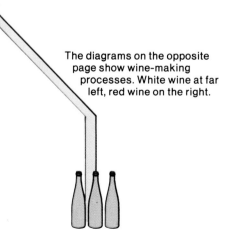

The diagrams on the opposite page show wine-making processes. White wine at far left, red wine on the right.

Rosé wine gets its color from grape skins allowed to ferment with grape juice for a short time.

Tasting Wine

Wine tasters have a habit of using elaborate phrases to describe their favorite wines. One well-known example is summed up in a James Thurber cartoon with the caption:

"It is a naive domestic Burgundy without any breeding, but I think you'll be amused by its presumption."

The trick to wine tasting is to ignore the fancy phrases. I suggest you use a small notebook to record your impressions of different wines. Take the notebook with you when you dine out or go to wine-tasting parties. Write down everything you can think of about the wine, even if it seems trivial. For example, if a white Burgundy reminds you of your dog after it has been out on a wet day, write it down. Memory is the key to wine-tasting, and notes like these help to jog your memory when you consider trying that same wine again. Refer to the notebook when buying wine.

Traditionally, the wine taster divides his notes into the following categories.

1) Observe the color and carity of the wine by viewing it in front of light. Color helps indicate the age of the wine.

2) Swirl the wine in the glass to release the bouquet.

A silver *tastevin* is used by professional wine tasters. It is small, unbreakable, and shows the color of the wine well.

APPEARANCE

The wine taster will ask, "Is the wine clear and bright, and what is its color?" White wines can be slightly greenish, a pale yellow, deep gold, or similar. Red wines are often deep purple when young, becoming ruby or garnet. Even later they become brick-red color after aging in wooden casks. The older the wine—whether red, white or rosé—the browner it looks. Generally, young wines do not have a brown cast.

The color of a wine may remind you of jewels. A flawed wine, like a second-rate gem, is cloudy and not brilliant. Any sediment in a red wine should be settled in the bottom of the bottle. A white wine should never show sediment.

BOUQUET

The bouquet, or aroma, of a wine is the truest test of its quality. Classifying an aroma can be difficult. An unpleasant aroma implies a wine of dubious quality. A wine that was stored in musty old casks will smell like rotten mushrooms. A wine with a poor cork will smell like wet sawdust. The odor of rotten cabbage can mean that the wine maker was too liberal in his use of sulfur dioxide as a preservative.

Conversely, a subtle and pleasant scent promises a tasty wine. A fine

3) Smell the wine. The aroma will indicate if the wine has spoiled or promises a good flavor.

4) When tasting the wine, let the wine stay in your mouth for a while before you swallow it. Then note the aftertaste.

young French Beaujolais smells of rose petals. A vintage champagne like buttered toast. One French wine taster I overheard claimed that claret smells like an expensive fur coat.

TASTE

The taste of the wine should confirm its bouquet. If its aroma was fresh and fruity, it should taste slightly acidic. To detect acidity, think of lemon juice or a tart apple.

If the taste of a white wine is sharp enough to make your mouth pucker, it could have too much acid, or an excess of one type called *malic acid*. With red wines, mouth puckering means tannic acid. In time, this taste mellows and becomes less harsh as the wine ages. It blends in with the fruity flavor of the young wine.

Because there are few words to describe taste, be creative when describing a wine. If it is not sweet, sour or bitter, you will have to compare it with a familiar-tasting food or drink, or find more poetic expressions.

FINISH AND BALANCE

Both of these words are used by professional wine tasters to confound the ordinary drinker. *Finish* describes the taste remaining in your mouth after drinking wine. A heavy, alcoholic wine will be *rich* and *full-bodied*. The taste will stay with you for some time after swallowing. This is called a *long finish*.

Conversely, a *young, light* white wine such as a Mosel may have a delicious flavor that fades rapidly. The flavor of a wine that has grown old will disappear from your mouth quickly. A very young, coarse wine will have a powerful flavor but might spoil your appetite. These have a *short finish*.

The ideal wine is called *balanced*. This term implies the "right" combination of tannic acid, sweetness, fruit flavor, and other characteristics. Basically, it means that the wine is true to itself. For example, the true style of a Mosel wine is always fruity, low in alcohol, fresh and acidic. A good Mosel will have all these qualities, but none to excess—it will be balanced. An out-of-balance wine can have too much sugar, too much acid, too much tannin, too much alcohol, or a combination of these.

THE WINE-TASTING PARTY

A wine-tasting party is a good way to try many different wines of the world. It is great fun and an efficient way to learn about the qualities of many wines. Invite a small group of friends—they don't have to be experts. Ask each to bring a bottle, such as a favorite wine or one they want to try for the first time.

Having a theme to the party is useful. You can try white wines from one region, red wines from another, or compare French and California wines.

Always taste from dry to sweet. Try the youngest wines first, otherwise one wine may mask the flavor of the next.

See pages 20 and 21 for tips on serving wine. You may want to cover the labels and merely mark each bottle with a number. Evaluate each wine when you taste it and compare your impressions with those of your friends when you check your results against the label.

You don't have to spit out the wine after tasting each glass, but don't drink too much because it can dull the taste-buds. Smoking is not advisable because it hides the subtle scent of wine, as does strong perfume. Serve bread or unsalted crackers and water so you can cleanse your palate between tastes. Save the cheese and salad for later to accompany a chosen bottle or two.

Wine	Appearance (3)	Bouquet (5)	Taste (5)	Finish/ Balance (7)	Comments	Total (20)
California Cabernet Sauvignon 1980	Ruby color, bright. (3)	Fruity, rich. (4)	Full-bodied, velvety. (4)	Long finish, good balance. (6)	A well-made wine with several years to age.	17
Château Margaux 1975	Garnet color, bright. (3)	Complex, full bouquet. (4)	Powerful, dry. (4)	Long finish, fine balance. (7)	Exceptional wine with many years of life.	18

A *tasting card* like this one is a valuable record of the wines you've tasted. Score the wine in each category. The maximum points are shown under each heading. A superb wine rates 19 or 20 points. An inexpensive, well-balanced wine rates 16 or 17 points.

Glasses

As with wines, there are many styles of wine glasses available. Choosing the right glass for a certain wine lets you appreciate the way the wine looks. In some cases, it promotes a flavorful bouquet. In any case, the glass you select should complement the wine and enrich the wine-tasting experience.

TASTER'S GLASS

All wine glasses should be clear and without any engraving or etching. They should be made of glass or crystal as thin as possible, with a fine rim. So you can savor the bouquet of the wine, the shape of the glass should taper slightly toward the top. The stem should be long for holding the wine up to the light. The base should be solid for setting down the glass.

A typical tasting glass holds about 10 fluid ounces when full. However, no wine glass should ever be filled to the top because this would prevent you from swirling the wine in the glass to develop the bouquet.

DRINKER'S GLASS

There is no set size for any drinking glass. The average holds about 10 fluid ounces, but any size will do, provided the glass is clear and has a stem. With wine glasses that open out at the top into a trumpet shape, the fragrance of the wine is especially apparent, but does not last for long.

It is possible to use a tasting glass for drinking too, but many people prefer to have slightly larger glasses for drinking red wine, slightly smaller for white. The reason is that red wines respond to contact with the air, but white wines do not usually benefit from "breathing."

The rounded, balloon-shaped glass is used for serving Burgundy and similar full-bodied, dry red wines. German wines from the Rhine and Mosel are often offered in tall glasses with green or brown stems and small bowls. These are purely decorative.

Many people understandably choose fine crystal glasses for serving their best wines. The beauty of these glasses shows off a fine wine, but you should avoid cut crystal. The elaborate design hides the color of the wine. Use

The tulip-shaped champagne glass or *flûte* has a hollow stem, so bubbles last longer than they do in a saucer shaped *coupe*.

German wines are often served in glasses with this shape. Sometimes the glass is colored.

A balloon glass holds about twice as much wine as an average wine glass.

Traditionally, this glass is used for Alsatian wines.

Paris goblet is a simple glass ideal for everyday wine.

these for vermouth or sherry served with ice.

CHAMPAGNE GLASS

Traditionally, champagne for celebrations is served in flat dish-shaped glasses. This shape shows the bubbles well, but also means the bubbles will soon be gone. Better glasses are lovely *flûtes*, which are slim, tall glasses. Some flûtes have a diamond cut in the hollowed-out stem, causing the bubbles to rise in a single stream from that point.

APPETIZER WINES

Vermouth is served either straight in a simple wine glass, or over ice in a cocktail tumbler. Sherry can be served in a special, short-stemmed tapered glass that concentrates the bouquet of the drink. This isn't necessary if you serve sherry over ice in a small tumbler.

DESSERT WINES

Dessert wines like port and madeira are usually served in a short-stemmed glass with a smaller capacity than one used for table wines. Because dessert wines are very sweet, only a small amount is served. Fine, sweet white wines like Sauternes are also served in a small wine glass.

WASHING GLASSES

Many wine connoisseurs never allow detergent to come in contact with their tasting glasses. For tasting purposes, glasses are always washed with very hot water, then drained on a clean linen cloth or suspended in a rack to dry. Using a drying cloth may give glasses a hint of unwanted flavor. For everyday drinking glasses, however, dish-washing detergent is OK.

STORING GLASSES

Many tasters store their glasses sus-pended in racks above a sink, but glasses may also be stored on shelves in a cupboard. Be sure they are not stored near any polished wood or foods with strong flavors. These aromas can taint the flavor of the wine served in the glass.

Engraved, crystal glasses are attractive and elegant, but they are not always best if you want to appreciate a wine's clarity.

A traditional hock glass has a stout, knobbled stem of brown glass that reflects color into the pale wine.

A half-full copita is just right for sherry, port, madeira and other appetizer and dessert wines.

A taster's glass is also elegant enough for using at the table.

Storing Wine

If you observe some simple rules and conditions for storage, you can easily keep wines for a long time.

STORAGE CONDITIONS

An underground cellar is practical and attractive. However, few people today are lucky enough to own a cellar and must make do with a cupboard, closet, or corner of a garage that has the following conditions:

Temperature—A constant temperature of about 55F (13C) is ideal. A variable temperature between 45F and 65F (7C and 18C) is acceptable if the change is slow and steady.

Vibration—Minimize this because you don't want to stir up any sediment in the wine. Nor do you want the cork to loosen.

Darkness—Prolonged exposure to sunlight will warm up a bottle of wine. This is why darkness is usually recommended as a condition for storage. However, room lights will not affect a wine.

Humidity—Cool air is moist air, so if the temperature of your storage area is low, the humidity should be just right. Generally, humidity conditions that *you* find comfortable are OK for wine. The humidity should be moderate, neither dry nor damp, and consistent throughout the year.

For everyday drinking, keep red wines in a wine rack in your dining room or kitchen, and white wines in the refrigerator. When storing wines, lay them on their sides so the wine is in contact with the base of the cork. This prevents the cork from drying out and shrinking. A tight-fitting cork does not allow air to enter the wine and age it prematurely.

WINE BINS AND RACKS

Some fine clarets and vintage ports are still shipped in wooden crates. You can use these as wine bins by turning them on their sides so the wine is lying on its side. Cardboard cartons are not suited to cellar storage because they can develop mold that may affect the wine through the cork. Also, they collapse if they become damp.

To avoid such problems, store your wines in a bin made from a wooden box. Lay the bottles sideways, stacked tightly in each box. Label each bin with a number or code and keep a record of the wine in each.

A wine rack can be either wood or metal. Some small, ornate racks are intended for the dining room, while others may be built to hold dozens of bottles. These can be attached to the wall of a cellar or closet. Place bottles in the rack with the label on top. This avoids damaging the labels and allows you to read them without disturbing the wine.

CELLAR BOOK

You can keep a cellar book of your own as a record of what you have and have already consumed. Special books are available at wine stores. Record each wine and your impressions of it.

From left to right: Wicker wine carrier for 8 bottles, Wine rack for 12 bottles, candle for decanting wine, cellar book.

YOUR HOME SUPPLY

It's convenient to divide your purchases into two types—wines for everyday drinking and wines for special occasions. These types of wines are described in more detail in other sections of this book.

EVERYDAY DRINKING

Wines in this category can include ordinary table or *jug* wines—generally sold in half- or full-gallon bottles. These need no cellar aging. Otherwise, choose about two dozen bottles from the following types:

Fruity White Wines—Include Liebfraumilch, Yugoslav Riesling, California Colombard and Chenin Blanc, Alsace Sylvaner, Australian Rhine Riesling.

Dry White Wines—Include French Muscadet and White Bordeaux, Italian Frascati and Verdicchio, California Sauvignon Blanc and Australian Semillon.

Light Red Wines—Include French Beaujolais and inexpensive claret, Gamay from California, and rosé from Portugal, France or California.

Full-Bodied Red Wines—Include California Zinfandel, Australian Shiraz, Mâcon Rouge and Côtes du Rhône from France, Italian Chianti and Spanish Rioja.

SPECIAL OCCASIONS

You can choose fine wines for special occasions with some help from your local wine dealer. Keep them in good condition for the recommended times. If you don't want to store a wine, you may have to pay more for it when it is at its peak.

Fine White Wines—Drink these within about five years of production, the year shown on the bottle's label. Dry white wines include Chablis from France, white Burgundy, German Rhine and Mosel wines, and Alsatian wines.

Sweet White Wines—These will keep for a long time. French Sauternes and German Beerenauslese and Trockenbeerenauslese wines can last for 50 years or longer. Generally, your fine, sweet white wines will be at their best within five to 10 years from the date of the vintage.

Fine Red Wines—Unless your wine is from one of the finest vintages, drink claret, Burgundy and good red wines from California, Australia and South Africa within five to 10 years after the vintage date.

Wines that you should keep longer, up to 20 years, include: Barolo and other Italian wines made with the Nebbiolo grape; full-bodied Rhône wines; and some California wines that are heavy and high in alcoholic content.

Sparkling Wines—When champagne and other sparkling wines are sold, they have completed their aging process and are ready for drinking.

Fortified Wines—This is a strong, sometimes sweet, wine with an alcoholic content of about 20%. Almost all fortified wines, including sherry, port and Marsala, are ready for drinking and do not need to be stored for aging. Vintage port needs at least 10 years in a cellar before it is ready to drink.

Serving Wine

Different types of wine are available to be enjoyed before, during and after a meal. There are many rules and conventions about serving wine with food. The most important consideration when serving any wine is to choose one you will enjoy. See pages 104 to 107 about appetizer and dessert wines.

Luncheon Wines—These should complement the food, not overpower it. As a general rule, serve lighter, drier wines before heavier, sweeter wines. Also, a young wine should normally be served before an older one.

Soups, Salads and Appetizers—Consider a light, dry wine, such as Riesling, Chablis, Muscadet or Semillon. A full-flavored meat or chicken soup may be accompanied by a dry sherry.

Fish—Serve a dry white wine like Chablis, Muscadet, Sauvignon Blanc from California or any similar acidic wine.

Strong fish stews, such as *Cioppino* or *Bouillabaisse* are rich in tomato and garlic. These taste wonderful with a light red wine such as a California Burgundy or a red wine from Southwest France.

Chicken and White Meat—Serve these with either red or white wine. If you are using a cream sauce over the meat, a white Burgundy or Semillon is a good accompaniment. With roasted meat or Italian-style dishes, serve a red wine such as Beaujolais or Chianti.

Red Meat and Game—These taste good with all fine red wines. A steak is traditionally served with good claret. Red Burgundy goes well with roast beef. For venison and other flavorful game, try the full-bodied Rhône red wines, like Hermitage or an Australian Shiraz. Barbecued meats require a full-flavored wine like California Petite Sirah or Zinfandel.

Some Taboos—Although there are no rigid rules about serving wines with food, avoid the following combinations. Otherwise, the result is an unpleasant taste in your mouth.

- Mackerel or any oily fish and red wine.
- Chocolate and any wine.
- Vinaigrette salad dressing with any wine.
- Lemon desserts and any wine.
- Rich egg dishes and white wine.

WINE AT THE TABLE

After deciding on the wines to accompany a meal, the next step is to prepare them for the meal. This puts them in peak condition for drinking.

Temperature—Red wines taste best when served at a temperature between 65F and 70F (18C to 21C), sometimes called *cellar temperature*. What we consider *room temperature* is often too warm, about 72F (22C). This can dull the full flavor of a good red wine. If necessary, chill the wine briefly to lower its temperature near 68F (20C). The exception to this rule is a Beaujolais or Gamay. Both taste better when chilled like a white wine.

White wines require chilling before opening. Generally, a two-hour chill is enough, but some people like their white wine a bit colder or a bit warmer. It is better to serve it colder, because the wine will always warm up after it is poured. If necessary, you can chill a white wine in the freezer for 20 to 30 minutes before serving. Don't forget about the bottle. You can expect it to explode if it freezes. Some people keep a bottle of white wine chilled at the table by putting it in an ice bucket filled with ice and water.

Champagne should be chilled to about 45F (7C) to ensure that the bubbles are released slowly and the flavor retained. Use an ice bucket filled with ice and water to keep the temperature down while the bottle is at the table.

Opening the Bottle—Always use a corkscrew to remove the bottle's cork. Corkscrews come in a multitude of shapes and sizes. Each wine drinker has his favorite. Be sure the screw part is long and curled enough to get a grip on the whole cork. Otherwise, the cork could break and fall into the wine.

To open champagne, hold the cork with your thumb while twisting the bottle firmly in one direction to release the pressure *slowly!* This way you won't lose precious gas and flavor in an explosive, frothy pop.

Breathing—Some experts recommend that you let a wine *breathe* before you pour it. What you do is remove the cork and let the bottle sit undisturbed before pouring it. The reaction of the air with the wine is said to affect the taste of the wine.

Some people let a white wine breathe for about 10 minutes. They claim that it makes a fresh, young wine taste less acidic.

Letting a red wine breathe is more confusing. If the wine is very old, letting it breathe too much can ruin it! Avoid such a problem by tasting the wine after opening it. If it is not harsh, recork it and serve it without benefit of breathing. Otherwise, sample it every

30 minutes. Don't let it breathe for more than two hours. For younger wines, a breathing time from 30 minutes to one hour is usually sufficient.
Decanting—This is pouring the wine into another serving container, such as an attractive crystal decanter. This is useful if you are serving a red wine that has sediment in the bottom of the bottle. Before decanting, let the bottle stand upright for an hour or two. Then pour the wine slowly into the decanter. With a candle or light

From left to right:
Wine carrier for a single bottle, corkscrew,
ship's decanter,
decantavin, a device for decanting wine,
taster's glass.

behind the bottle, watch for the sediment. When it reaches the neck of the bottle, stop pouring.
Pouring—Pour a little wine into the host's glass first. Let him test its quali-ty. Then serve from each person's right. Move clockwise around the table. A standard size bottle of wine—about 25.5 fluid ounces—will serve four to six people.

2

CHOOSING WINE

Choosing Bar at the Folies Bergères by
Edouard Manet (1832-1883). Courtauld
Institute, London.

Wines of France

When many people all over the world think of wine, they first think of France. Drinking French wine is like drinking history. Almost 10% of the population of France is connected with the wine business. Much of the annual production consists of ordinary red table wine, *vin ordinaire*, which is most enjoyable when consumed young and fresh.

Some French wines are made at grand *chateâux*, castled estates owned by titled families. Some are made in the *caves* or cellars of the *négociants*, wine merchants who also bottle wines. Small, local growers who don't have wine-making facilities usually send their crops to regional cooperatives to be crushed and fermented, then sold as wine on their behalf.

FRENCH WINE LAWS

At the end of the 19th century, the French wine industry was recovering from a disastrous infestation of a vine louse that destroyed most vineyards. Unscrupulous wine makers were labeling their wines fraudulently. To protect her international reputation, the French government stepped in and created strict laws that controlled various aspects of the industry. Some of the most important ones that help you identify wines are described here.

Appellation Contrôlée (AC)—All fine French wines come from areas controlled by a government body called the *Institut National des Appellations d'Origine (INAO)*. This institute establishes the naming (*appellation*) system for each wine district. Under its guidance, wine makers conform to rules that specify how many vines may be grown per acre, how much wine may

Château Lynch-Bages;
Rosé d'Anjou;
Pouilly-Fuissé 1979;
Veuve Clicquot Ponsardin, Brut;
Bollinger 1975 in champagne bucket.

be made from each acre of vines, and the minimum amount of alcohol in the wine.

About 15% of all French wines are *appellation contrôlee*, coming from areas recognized as producers of top-quality wines. This title is clearly marked on the bottle's label, sometimes with the initials *AC*. Also on the label is the date of the vintage, or year of the grape harvest from which the wine was made.

Vins Délimités de Qualité Supérieur (VDQS)—Wines with the initials *VDQS* on the label are considered good, well-made wines from a particular small region. To win the *VDQS* seal a producer must conform to a set of regulations almost as rigorous as those for the *AC*.

Vin de Pays—Literally, this means *country wine*. They are simple wines that represent the characteristic style of a particular region, which is sometimes named on the bottle.

Vin de Marque—This is wine with a brand name, chosen by the shipper or cooperative that makes the wine. The purpose is to offer the customer a reliable wine that does not vary from year to year. These are usually not vintage-dated because they can be made from blends of wines from different years.

OTHER WORDS YOU'LL SEE ON FRENCH LABELS

Blanc: White.
Cépage: Grape type.
Château: Estate.
Commune: Village or township after which a wine is named.
Demi-sec: Medium-sweet.
Doux: Sweet.
Mise en bouteilles au château: Estate-bottled.
Mousseux: Sparkling. It is used for wines other than champagne.
Propriétaire: Owner of the property and wine-making business.
Récolte, millésime: Vintage.
Rouge: Red.
Sec: Dry.
Supérieur: This usually means the wine is more alcoholic than the ordinary local wine.
Vendange tardive: Late-harvest grapes.

BORDEAUX

This region in the western part of France produces more *appellation côntrollée (AC)* wine than any other part of France. Wines of every style are made here. The Médoc, a flat area north of the city of Bordeaux, is famed for dry red wines known to many people as *claret*. This name is derived from an old French word *clairet,* meaning light in color. Médoc wines are usually paler than red wines from Burgundy.

Due south of Bordeaux is the region where Sauternes are made. These delicious, sweet wines are made by an elaborate method involving selecting bunches of grapes by hand. All around the surrounding area are famous *appellations,* from crisp, dry whites to full-bodied reds.

GRAPE VARIETIES

The region produces equal quantities of white and red wine. However, most of the fine wines are red. Many white wines are *vin ordinaires* and are not exported.

Bordeaux offers many kinds of wines because of different soil conditions in the region. A particular soil is best for a certain grape variety. For example, the fine red Médoc wines are produced from grapes grown on deep gravel beds, which drain water well. Likewise, the Graves region is named after its gravelly soil.

In the Sauternes, the fine white wines are produced from grapes grown on a layer of limestone deposited over gravel. St. Emilion, another good red-wine *appellation,* has more clay mixed into the soil. This gives the wines pungent flavors and a so-called "earthy" taste.

In Bordeaux, the main red-wine grapes include Cabernet Sauvignon, Merlot, Cabernet Franc, Malbec and Petit Verdot. The first three are more important than the others. Cabernet Sauvignon is considered the finest in flavor, but Merlot ripens earlier and has a softer taste. Cabernet Franc makes a lighter, simpler wine.

Most fine clarets are blends of all three in quantities that vary from château to château and from year to year. Because the weather in this area can be poor in spring and early summer, it is common for some grapes to be damaged or ruined. In these poor vintages, lighter wines are made with the grapes that remain.

The white wine grapes are Sauvignon Blanc, Semillon and Muscadelle. The first two are fine varieties. Muscadelle is not used much today. All three may be used to make dry or sweet white wines.

MÉDOC

Most connoisseurs agree that this region produces the most complex,

Château Coutet, Barsac 1974;
Château du Biac 1977;
Château Lagrange 1973;
Château de Millegrand 1978.

subtle and distinguished red wines of Bordeaux. All the fine wines are classified according to quality from a list created during an evaluation in 1855. This divided them into five categories of production, or *cru.* A *cru classé* is a classified wine from this list. A *premier cru classé* is a first-rate wine produced in the region. A *deuxième cru classé* is second, and so on. This is usually printed on the label.

It is important to remember when choosing a wine from this district that the classification can be out of date. Some wines, such as Château Lynch-Bages, were originally classified fifth (*cinquième cru classé*), but today command prices as high as those for those classified second. When in doubt about the actual quality of a *cru classé* wine, consult your wine dealer.

Below this category are several other classes of wine, all of them of good quality, sometimes equal to the more expensive *cru classés.* Some are *cru exceptionnel, cru bourgeois supérieur,* and *cru bourgeois.*

Some wines are named after the particular village, or *commune,* of origin. The great Médoc communes are St. Es-

tèphe, Pauillac, St. Julien, and Margaux. Wine that does not come from one particular château, like the *crus classés*, or one commune, may be named after the district, such as in Médoc and Haut Médoc. The *haut* in Haut Médoc indicates that the wine is from the top-quality region of the Médoc.

Any wine called *Bordeaux* or *Bordeaux Supérieur* may come from anywhere within the region, and is probably a blended wine of average quality.

ST. EMILION AND POMEROL

The rich, full red wines of these areas have an enthusiastic following. Château Petrus, the top Pomerol wine, fetches the highest price of any Bordeaux wine.

St. Emilion wines are classified like those of the Médoc. They are divided into *premier grand cru classé*, the top rank, and *grand cru classé*. Below these are many wines confusingly labeled *grand cru*—some of which are not too good—others are excellent. Pomerol wines have never been classified, but some are called *grand vin* anyway. The title is well-deserved in most cases.

GRAVES

Graves does not produce white wines exclusively. In fact, Château Haut Brion, classified as a *premier cru*, is considered as fine a red wine as any in the Médoc. However, the dry and medium-sweet white wines of the Graves are the best known. They have an unusual metallic flavor, described as the opposite of fruity, which some experts call "steely."

SAUTERNES AND BARSAC

Rich, sweet white wines from these regions are produced by a very special natural process. Few areas in the world can duplicate it because it requires a special combination of climate and a mold called *botrytis cinerea*. This mold forms on the ripe grapes and penetrates the skins. The hot sun evaporates the water and concentrates the juice. Each bunch affected by the *pourriture noble* (noble rot) is handpicked and pressed daily. This makes a rich, sweet wine with a honey-like flavor.

Although the taste is sweet, the aftertaste is dry. Naturally this process is expensive and the yield small. These special wines are worth trying.

Sauternes are classified in a similar way to Médoc wines.

ENTRE-DEUX-MERS AND PREMIÈRS CÔTES DE BORDEAUX

These two areas produce large quantities of ordinary dry and medium-sweet white wine. The best-known red wine is labeled *Bordeaux Supérieur*.

BURGUNDY

The heart of Burgundy is contained in an area called the Côte d'Or, about 270 miles southeast of Paris. Lovers of fine Burgundy will pay any price for a bottle of their favorite Burgundian *cru*. Critics claim that the rarity of some wines has led to merchants charging inflated prices for them.

One straightforward explanation for the high prices is that the vineyards are very small and the region is so far north as to make the climate unpredictable.

Many people own small vineyards in Burgundy. Each vineyard is called a *climat*. It usually forms part of a larger *domaine*, or property. In addition to the *proprietaire récoltant*, the property owner who makes wine himself, there are many *négociants* who blend and sell wines from their cellars. They are usually located in a large town like Beaune.

Because the wine-making activity in Burgundy is much more complex than in Bordeaux, some people choose their wines according to the name of the vineyard. However, there are so many producers that it is best to rely on the name of the shipper when searching for a quality wine. The name of the shipper is usually printed on the label.

Some well-known Burgundy shippers include Louis Latour, Jadot, Joseph Drouhin, Bouchard Père et Fils, Chanson, Patriarche, Charles Vienot, and Jaboulet-Vercherre. Wines exported by these firms represent the particular qualities of the *commune* or *climat* named on the label.

GRAPE VARIETIES

The Côte d'Or is usually divided into two separate districts—Côte de

Nuits, famous for red wines, and Côte de Beaune, famous for white wines. The entire area is in the form of a ridge, consisting mainly of limestone. There is some clay mingling with the limestone soil in the Côte de Nuits.

The Côte de Beaune is purer limestone, with chunks of chalk scattered over the soil. These are ideal conditions for certain grape varieties to flourish. Wine makers all over the world seek out similar soil to cultivate similar vines in the hope that they can make their own "Burgundies."

The Pinot Noir grape is used to make the robust red wines. For white wines the Chardonnay grape is used. Both are delicate varieties that cannot yield heavy crops. The yield is strictly controlled by the *INAO,* so each vineyard earns the right to the *AC* of that area.

Côte de Beaune 1978;
Meursault 1977;
Nuits-St.-Georges 1978;
Pommard Epenots 1971.

CÔTE DE BEAUNE

Pommard is a "velvety" red wine made in a commune on the Côte de Beaune. Despite its well-deserved reputation, it is not the finest red wine of the area. That distinction belongs to Le Corton. Any Burgundy with *Le* plus the *appellation* is the finest of its category. Lesser wines have longer versions of the name, such as Aloxe-Corton.

In addition to the good but often overpriced Pommard, other communes in the Beaune region are Beaune, Pernand-Vergelesses, Aloxe-Corton, and Savigny-les-Beaune. When choosing a wine from this illustrious area, rely on the name and reputation of the shipper to guide you. Some names are mentioned earlier. Most of them are based in the attractive medieval town of Beaune.

Two famous names in white Burgundy are Montrachet and Meursault. Although these communes are very close to each other on the Côte de Beaune, their wines are distinctly different. Montrachet is considered subtle and complex. Meursault tastes heavier and has a buttery flavor.

Fine wines with similar characteristics to Le Montrachet include Chevalier Montrachet, Bâtard Montrachet and Puligny Montrachet. The next level down from these elegant wines are those labeled *premier cru.* They are also slightly lower in price than the *grands crus.* Wines with just a commune name and no vineyard mentioned on the label are the best values.

CÔTE DE NUITS

This area includes many famous communes. To the north are Fixin, Gevrey Chambertin, Chambolle-Musigny and Vougeot. From each comes a memorable red wine, notably Le Musigny and Le Chambertin.

To the south of these is the best known village of all — Vosne-Romanée. A mere four acres of land here produce the legendary *crus* of Romanée Conti. One special feature of the vineyards is that they escaped the ravages of the vine louse *phylloxera,* which destroyed essentially all European vineyards in the 19th century. Romanée-Conti can therefore boast pre-*phylloxera* vines.

The major *crus* here are called Romanée-Conti, La Tâche, Romanée St. Vivant, and Richebourg. Close by is the town of Nuits St. Georges, a commune name you'll find on many pleasant red Burgundies.

Vin ordinaire of Burgundy bears the *appellation Bourgogne,* either *Blanc* or *Rouge.* Although these are variable in quality, sometimes they are good.

BEAUJOLAIS, CHABLIS & MÂCON

The wines of the Côte d'Or are full-bodied, rich and meant to keep well. The wines of these three regions are best when drunk young. With very few exceptions the red and white wines of these regions surrounding the Burgundy vineyards are made in a light, fresh style that will fade within 10 years, or sooner.

GRAPE VARIETIES

Beaujolais produces about 15 million gallons of red wine each year. This prolific output is partly explained two ways. The soil is granitic, so it is less austere than the harsh limestone of the Côte d'Or. Another reason is the different grape—the Gamay. Wines made from this grape are usually light in color and fragrant, with a scent like rose petals or strawberries.

The village of Chablis is perched on a limestone outcrop to the north of the Côte d'Or. Unlike fertile, southern Beaujolais, this cool area cannot make enough white wine to supply demand. Low-yielding Chardonnay grapes are used. The fine wines must conform to AC restrictions on production.

Like Beaujolais, the Mâcon area lies to the south of Burgundy, toward Lyon. The soil varies here. There is one fine limestone region that is the home of Pouilly-Fuissé, but the other white wines of Mâcon are produced on granitic soils. The better white wines including Pouilly-Fuissé are made with the Chardonnay grape. Some are labeled with the grape variety used to distinguish them from other wines made with the Aligoté, an ordinary white grape. Most red wines are made from the Gamay grape, although some Pinot Noir grapes are grown here.

The best red wines of Beaujolais bear the name of a particular commune. Nine villages are allowed to name wines according to *AC* regulations—Chenas, Chiroubles, Côte de Brouilly, Brouilly, Fleurie, Julienas, Saint Amour, Morgon, and Moulin-à-Vent.

All produce excellent wines in good years. The finest of all are generally accepted to be Moulin-à-Vent and Morgon. These two improve with age and may be kept for up to 10 years. The others are best when consumed from five to eight years after vintage.

In addition to the village wines with special names, certain wines are simply called *Beaujolais Villages*. This means that the wine is a blend of various good-quality barrels from several villages.

Wine labeled *Beaujolais* with no mention of the village can be very good when the vintage is fine, or poor in a bad year. When in doubt, ask your wine dealer.

Demand for Beaujolais is so great that a large amount is now sold from less successful vineyards. If you do not recognize the name of the shipper as a reputable one, treat the wine with caution. Names to look for on Beaujolais labels include Piat, Mommessin, George Duboeuf, Bouchard Aîné, and Reynier.

Each November a very young, new Beaujolais is made available amid a fanfare of publicity. This is *Beaujolais Primeur*, also known as *Nouveau* (new). The French also call it the *vin de l'année*, or wine of the new year. This is a light, almost fizzing, pale red wine that should be consumed before the New Year.

CHABLIS

The district of Chablis is about halfway between Paris and the Côte d'Or. Many wine connoisseurs prize its white wine, Chablis, above almost any other. It has an intensely dry, almost harsh flavor called "flinty" by professional tasters. It seems to taste of the chalk that gave it birth.

The finest Chablis are from *grand cru* vineyards. Next is *premier cru*, then the simple *appellation* Chablis without a named vineyard. Lesser wines are appropriately called *Petit Chablis*. Because of the worldwide demand for Chablis, none are inexpensive.

MÂCON

The success story of this area south of the Côte d'Or is the wine Pouilly-Fuissé. Like Pommard from the Côte de Beaune, this is a fashionable wine. Therefore, it can be overpriced and hard to find. In this case, consider other good dry white wines from the Mâcon. These include Pouilly-Vinzelles and Saint Veran. Be careful not to confuse Pouilly-Fuissé with Pouilly Fumé. The latter is an entirely different wine from the Loire valley.

Wines with Mâcon in their names can vary in quality, so it is worth knowing the name of the shipper when choosing. Look for the same shippers mentioned in the Beaujolais section.

Mâcon Vire, Mâcon Prisse and Mâcon Lugny are white wines named after a particular village. These can be excellent wines. Red wines called Mâcon Rouge are less interesting, but reasonably priced, pleasant everyday wines.

Chablis 1979;
Pouilly-Fuissé 1979;
Beaujolais Pisse-Dru 1980;
Morgon 1979.

CHAMPAGNE

Throughout the world, the name *champagne* is used to mean a particular type of wine—an elegant, sparkling, and expensive liquid used for celebrations. The wine makers of Champagne are dismayed by this. To them, and the laws of France, champagne is a very special sparkling wine made according to age-old traditions in one small part of France, northeast of Paris near Reims.

GRAPE VARIETIES

The northern vineyards of the Champagne region have never made good wine. The Chardonnay, the grape variety for white Burgundies, and its sister grape, the Pinot Noir, do well on the limestone soils of Champagne. However, they rarely ripen fully to develop a rich, balanced flavor. The answer to this problem was to make a special type of wine—one with sparkle.

THE CHAMPAGNE METHOD

The idea of a sparkling wine was familiar to wine makers in Champagne from the earliest days of Roman occupation. During the warm days of spring, yeast in wine made in the previous autumn would begin fermenting again after the long cold winter. This *secondary fermentation* often left carbon dioxide bubbles in the wine. Many wine makers tried to eliminate this because sometimes the corked bottles exploded.

Some thought the sparkle in the wine improved it. For them, the problems were how to control the secondary fermentation and how to keep the bubbles in the bottle. According to legend, the first man to solve both problems was Dom Pérignon, cellarmaster of the Hautvillers Abbey near Epernay in the Champagne region.

He transferred the newly fermented wine to bottles and added yeast and sugar. He corked each bottle and set it aside in a cool cellar until a secondary fermentation took place. The added yeast and sugar encouraged a vigorous secondary fermentation, creating a lot of carbon dioxide gas. Because the bottle was tightly corked, the gas could not escape. Instead, it dissolved into the wine, waiting to bubble up when the bottle was opened.

To seal the bottles tightly, Dom Pérignon invented the modern style of champagne cork and tied it down into position. He also pioneered the use of strong bottles able to withstand the severe pressure created inside the bottle.

Thus champagne was born. Several years of aging after the secondary fermentation lent additional flavor and character, as the young champagne rested on the *lees,* the sediment of spent yeast cells. One final problem remained, and Dom Pérignon did not have an answer to this—how to remove the sediment without clouding the champagne?

Another process was invented by Veuve Clicquot to solve this problem. Madame Clicquot, who ran champagne behind the British lines during the Napoleonic Wars, was the widow of a champagne maker. Her process, called *rémuage,* involves a gradual turning of each bottle during upside-down storage. The sediment gradually sinks as a plug in the neck of the bottle. The cork is removed and the sediment poured out. The bottle is recorked.

This method is called *méthode champenoise.* Even today each stage is done by hand with painstaking skill and care. Naturally, this involves much time and money, making the price of fine champagne inevitably high.

CHAMPAGNE TYPES

All true champagne is made by the same method. The differences between champagnes occur during bottling. Today, the lees is removed by freezing the neck of the bottle. When the cork is removed, the frozen sediment and a small amount of frozen champagne

Moët & Chandon;
Bollinger 1975;
Veuve Clicquot-Ponsardin, Brut 1973.

goes with it. Then a small amount of old wine mixed with cane sugar, the *dosage,* is added, depending on the sweetness required of the final wine. This is necessary because all of the natural sugars were consumed during fermentations. If no *dosage* were added, a very dry champagne would result.

The types of champagnes most widely available include:

Brut—Very dry, with typical *dosage* of 0.5%.

Extra Dry—Not as dry as Brut, with typical *dosage* between 1 and 2%.

Demi-Sec—Slightly sweet and dry, with typical *dosage* between 4 and 6%.

Doux—Sweet, with typical *dosage* between 8 and 10%.

Pink Champagne—This is made by blending in a bit of local red wine for color. It is made in small quantities in the village of Bouzy.

One interesting aspect of all French champagnes is that most are made from a high proportion of black grapes, pressed so no color is extracted from the skins. The grapes used are the Pinot Noir and Pinot Meunier. Some wine from the white Chardonnay is also blended into a mixture of wines that become champagne. This mixture is called the *cuvée*. Some special champagnes you may see include:

Blanc de Blancs—Only white Pinot Chardonnay grapes are used. It is considered very delicate and fine.

Blanc de Noirs—This is a connoisseur's champagne made from only the black Pinot Noir. It is heavier than a Blanc de Blancs.

Crémant—Due to the use of less yeast and sugar in the secondary fermentation, there is less sparkle in this champagne than the regular type

Vintage-Dated Champagne—Champagne with a date printed on the label usually costs more than non-vintage types. This is because it has been chosen by the champagne maker to be aged for a longer period in his cellars. Vintage champagne is made only in good years, not every harvest.

CHAMPAGNE HOUSES

There are many famous names associated with champagne. Good champagne is also made by small independent growers and cooperatives. However most champagne available for export comes from a few top *maisons*, or houses. These include Bollinger, Krug, Lanson, Veuve Clicquot-Ponsardin, Pol Roger, Taittinger, Moët & Chandon, Heidsieck Monopole, Perrier-Jouët, Laurent Perrier, and Piper-Heidsieck.

LOIRE VALLEY

There are no really great and noble wines from the lovely château country of Western France. Nevertheless, the Loire region does offer a variety of good, lower-priced wines. These vineyards tend to produce wines of relatively low alcoholic content with a delicate flavor. Many are particularly good with fish dishes.

Probably the most famous wine from the Loire Valley is the rosé from Anjou, closely followed by white Vouvray and Sancerre. Muscadet is a Loire wine too, but it is from the extreme western part of the vineyards near the Atlantic Ocean.

GRAPE VARIETIES

To the west are the Muscadet vineyards around Nantes. Muscadet and Gros Plant grape varieties are planted here and give their names to the dry white wines produced. Labeling a wine after the grape used is unusual in France.

Moving east into Anjou and Touraine, most of the vines are grown on the gravelly and sheltered river banks. The major white grape is the Chenin Blanc, known here as the Pineau de la Loire. Chenin Blanc makes dry white wine, medium-dry white wines, and even sweet wines when affected by the noble rot *botrytis cinerea*.

For rosé wines and the few red wines of the Loire, the chief variety is the Cabernet Franc, which is also grown in Bordeaux. The Gamay grape is also used for rosé.

Pouilly Fumé 1978;
Rosé d'Anjou;
Muscadet 1979;
Vouvray 1979.

MUSCADET

This wine is invariably dry and acidic. Some Muscadet is labeled *sur lie*, which means it has been left on the lees to gain additional flavor before bottling. It is best within two years after being bottled.

ANJOU

The famous rosé from this area is labeled Rosé d'Anjou. It may be dry or medium-sweet. Some rosé wines are called *vin gris*, meaning they are exceptionally pale and made with particular care. The finest rosé is Cabernet Rosé, a full, deep pink wine made only from the Cabernet Franc grape.

In certain years Chenin Blanc grapes are affected by *botrytis cinerea*, the mold responsible for sweet Sauternes. Names to look for include Côteaux du Layon, Savennières, and Quarts de Chaume. These sweet wines have a honey-like fragrance.

SAUMUR

Rosé and white wines of Saumur are light and pleasant. A sparkling wine is also made with the *méthode champenoise*. It is usually dry and light.

Near Saumur are Chinon and Bourgeuil, two towns that make light, nutty red wines from the Cabernet Franc grape. These wines are best consumed young and fresh.

VOUVRAY

This famous wine name comes from the heart of the Château country. Here the Chenin Blanc grapes grow in chalky soil to produce a delicate and subtle wine said to taste of almonds and honey. In a good sunny year the wine may be sweet, especially if the grape is affected by *botrytis cinerea*. But in years that do not have enough sun, the wine becomes light and more acidic. Some is made into pleasant sparkling wine. The neighboring commune of Montlouis makes similar wines.

POUILLY AND SANCERRE

The current worldwide preference for dry white wines makes the prices for Chablis and white Burgundy rise ever higher. As these become costly, less-expensive wines from this area are increasingly popular. They are made from Sauvignon Blanc grapes, the type also grown in the Bordeaux region. The chalky soil gives the wine a hard-edged flavor, called "flinty." This has led some wine connoisseurs to call these wines "the poor man's Chablis."

Don't confuse the fruity, spicy Pouilly Fumé white wine with Pouilly-Fuissé from Mâcon. Both are dry white wines but are not similar in flavor. Pouilly-Fuissé is made with Chardonnay grapes and has a softer taste.

Other wines from the village Pouilly-sur-Loire are white wines blended from Sauvignon Blanc and Chasselas grapes. These wines are recognized by the name of the village on the label. Generally, their taste is less distinctive than the Pouilly Fumé wine.

Wine from Sancerre has become very popular and expensive. It is greenish-yellow and has the distinctive "bell-pepper" aroma of the Sauvignon Blanc grape. It is best when consumed three to four years after vintage.

RHÔNE VALLEY

Although the Rhône Valley has a varied terrain, the wines from the many villages resemble each other. The vines begin just below Lyon and are cultivated down the Rhône river valley as far as Avignon, the historic summer residence of the renegade French popes.

Every style of wine is made here. Red wines of the Rhône are more famous than the white. Because the Rhône is in the south of France, the climate is very hot. The vines also contend with fierce Mistral winds that howl along the valley. These conditions are extreme for most grapes. Only a few resistant types of white grapes grow. Some unusual red grapes thrive here.

GRAPE VARIETIES

The principal grape varieties of the region are Syrah, a red grape, and Viognier, a white grape. However, about 15 other types of grapes are also grown. The Syrah makes spicy, full red wines with a smell of black pepper. Under the name Shiraz it grows successfully in Australia and South Africa. It is known in California as the Petite Sirah. The Syrah grape thrives in hot regions.

The southern Rhône vineyards are steeply terraced. Large, flat pebbles lie on the ground, absorbing heat that is radiated toward the vines.

The Viognier grape does best in the northern Rhône Valley, growing in granitic soil. The most famous wine made with this grape is Condrieu. This grape also produces Château Grillet, the smallest *appellation* of France.

Other widely grown white grape varieties include the Rousanne and Marsanne, which make White Hermitage and other wines. These grapes are also used in the blend for Châteauneuf-du-Pape.

In the south, Grenache is important. This grape makes both red and rosé wine. The rosé wines are considered very fine, and have a particularly attractive orange color. The Cinsault grape is also used to make rosé.

CÔTE RÔTIE

The Syrah grape is cultivated on the chalky slopes of this "roasted hillside" (*côte rotie*). The red wines are full-flavored and smell of violets. Most improve when stored for many years, making them connoisseur wines.

HERMITAGE

As you move south along the Rhône, you'll see that the steep-sided hill of Hermitage is crowded with both red and white vines. From the Syrah grape, rich alcoholic red wines are made. These were highly prized in the 19th century. Today, people prefer a lighter wine that does not require as much aging before becoming drinkable. Hermitage wine makers are responding to this preference, making wines with less alcohol and tannic acid.

The white wines of Hermitage are made with the Viognier grape and are very distinctive. Their flavor is slightly oily, heavy and rich.

Red wines from vineyards on the lower slopes of the hill are named Crozes Hermitage. These are less expensive and distinguished than others from the same area.

CHÂTEAUNEUF-DU-PAPE

About five miles north of Avignon south of the Rhône Valley are the pebbly vineyards that produce Châteauneuf-du-Pape wines. Legally, wines called Châteauneuf-du-Pape may be made from a blend of up to 13 different grape varieties. This is a powerful, alcoholic wine, often reaching 16% in strength. When young, it is deep purple and tastes harsh. After 10 to 15 years of aging, it mellows and the flavor develops a spicy, warming quality. It is a classic winter wine.

As in Hermitage, some wine makers are making their Châteauneuf-du-Pape in a somewhat lighter style. Sadly, this can mean that some of the character is lost. You can also get dry and spicy white wines from Châteauneuf-du-Pape.

GIGONDAS

This area is close to Avignon and makes full-bodied, robust red wines in a style similar to those of Châteauneuf-du-Pape. Because the name is less well known than Châteauneuf-du-Pape, Gigondas wines can be good values.

TAVEL AND LIRAC

These south Rhône vineyards are famous for their distinctive orange-pink rosés, which are usually dry and alcoholic. Lirac also makes excellent full-bodied, rich red wine.

CÔTES DU RHÔNE

This *appellation* is sold everywhere in the world. Legally, it means that the wine is from the Rhône region. It may be a blend from wine of many areas or the excess production of a fine vineyard. The quality of these red, white and rosé wines is variable, so bargains are not always what they seem. Choose a Côtes du Rhône from a reliable shipper, such as Jaboulet or Delas, to get a top-quality wine.

Côtes du Rhône 1978;
Châteauneuf du Pape 1979;
Château du Trignon 1979.

ALSACE

Situated in the flat river valley of the Rhine and overshadowed by the Vosges mountains in northeast France, Alsace seems cut off from the rest of France. In fact, Alsace was part of Germany from 1870 to 1918. The wines reflect this. Some Alsatian wines are similar to the famous Rhine wines of Germany. They are made with similar grape varieties—but in a different way.

With few exceptions, the wines of Alsace are white, dry and intensely fruity. Unlike most other French wines, which are named after a village or vineyard, the wines of Alsace include the name of the grape variety.

Alsatian vineyards extend over about 70 miles, but only a small area produces top-quality wines. The picturesque medieval towns of Colmar, Riquewihr and Kaysersberg are at the center of this area. The vineyards spread from the towns into the foothills of the Vosges Mountains to heights of 600 to 1,200 feet. Although many slopes face east, the vines are sheltered from harsh weather by the flanks of the mountains. This allows the grapes to ripen well, sometimes giving rich, late-harvest wines.

Wine-making methods in Alsace are different from those in the rest of France. The fragrant white wines are made with grape varieties that can lose their subtle flavor if fermented too rapidly or if put into wooden casks. Therefore, Alsatian wine makers use a very long, cool fermentation that lasts several weeks. Eventually, the yeasts consume *all* of the grape sugar, yielding a totally dry wine. German wine

Gewurztraminer Hugel 1979;
Sylvaner Hugel 1978;
Edelwicker;
Pinot Blanc Hugel 1979.

makers use the same grape varieties, but stop the fermentation when some sugar remains in the wine.

Because all of the sugar is consumed in Alsatian wines, they have a relatively high alcoholic content—about 11%. This process also concentrates the flavor of the wine. Alsatian wines actually taste of the grape. Each different grape variety yields a truly distinctive wine suitable to accompany a particular food.

GRAPE VARIETIES

Many Alsatian wine makers consider wine from the white Riesling grape to be their finest and most delicate. It accompanies fish perfectly. Sylvaner is a closely related grape, making a light, dry, fragrant wine that is usually less expensive than the Riesling.

Gewürztraminer is a very strongly flavored wine—*gewürz* is German for

spicy. Its pungent flavor accompanies rich dishes like the local delicacy of fresh goose liver.

Most people think of wines made from Muscat grapes as sweet wines. In Alsace, however, they are "fermented to dryness," so the result is an unusually dry, spicy wine. It is rare and expensive.

Tokay d'Alsace is a rather confusing name for a grape also known as the Pinot Gris. It is not connected with the famous Tokay of Hungary. It is less spicy than some other Alsatian varieties, making a delicate *apéritif* wine.

Pinot Noir, the famous red grape of Burgundy, cannot ripen fully in Alsace, so wines from this grape are pale in color and not very interesting. Pinot Blanc makes light, dry white wines.

Any of the named grape types may appear on the labels of Alsatian wines, but the finer ones are known as the "noble varieties." These are the Riesling, Pinot Gris (Tokay), Muscat and Gewürztraminer. Wines made from noble grapes will naturally cost more. In addition, they may form part of a *grand cru*, or top-quality wine.

Only the noble grapes may be used for a *grand cru*. This title should not be confused with *grand vin*, which means only that the wine contains more than 11% alcohol. Noble grapes are also used to make a special blend called the *edelzwicker*, which in German means *noble mixture*.

Vendange tardive, or the German words *Auslese* and *Beerenauslese*, on a label means that the wine was made from very sweet, late-harvest grapes. This gives a sweet and expensive wine. Any noble variety may be used to make a *vendange tardive* wine, but the weather conditions are rarely good enough for such wines to succeed very often. They are made only in small quantities.

As with wines from other regions, if you know the name of reliable shippers, you have a good chance of getting a high-quality Alsatian wine. Some names include Hugel, Dopff and Irion, Trimbach, Leon Beyer and Schlumberger. These wines are never inexpensive, but their qualities are unmatched by any other French wines. They are not popular with the average wine drinker and deserve more recognition.

SOUTHWEST FRANCE

Most of the wines exported from France are *appellation contrôlée* wines from the well-known wine regions. In addition to these are many others that are not exported. Many are basic table wines made or blended in southern France.

The southwest of France has seemingly endless acres of undulating country. These acres are widely planted with vines, producing wines of all types. Few of them are famous, but many are well worth drinking. Because so few leave the country, you may have to visit France to appreciate these wines.

Much of all French wine is made in Languedoc-Rouissillon, but the name rarely appears on a label. Stretching across southern France from the Spanish border to the Rhône, this province includes the areas of Corbières, Minervois and Fitou. These names appear on inexpensive, well-made bottles of red wine.

GRAPE VARIETIES

Inland from Bordeaux are several areas that produce good-quality red, white and sparkling wines from a mixture of grape varieties, including those of Bordeaux and those of the Rhône.

The better wines of Languedoc-Roussillon are made from vines grown on high ground and stony slopes, where only vines or olive trees do well. Red grapes are definitely more successful than white because the climate is too hot for the more delicate white grapes.

The principal red grape varieties grown are the Grenache, Carignane, Cinsault and Mourvedre. These are traditional types that do well in the heat. Some experiments are also being done with plantings of Cabernet Sauvignon. And, California experts are advising the French wine makers about the cultivation of grapes in hot climates.

In hot climates like the South of France, central California and South Africa, red grape skins can become almost burnt, which gives a bitter flavor. One solution to this problem is to use a special fermentation method called *carbonic maceration*. Instead of crushing the grapes in the usual way, the wine makers put whole bunches in a sealed vat, where they ferment slowly. The result is a light, fruity red wine like Beaujolais.

LANGUEDOC-ROUSSILLON

This is one of the southern-most regions of France, near the balmy Mediterranean Sea. It is an ancient part of France that mainly produces robust red wines. These go well with spicy meats and cheeses.

Fitou AC—This dry, full-bodied red wine is one of the few *AC* wines of the region.

Corbières VDQS—Red wines from this area are gaining a reputation for reliable quality and value. Some even have grandiose château names on the labels, but don't be fooled. These wines may be well made and drinkable, but they will never be great. However, as claret prices climb higher, wines like these are reasonable substitutes.

Minervois VDQS—Like Corbières, this area lies in hilly country not far from the historic walled city of Carcassonne. Its dry red wines are similar to others of the region. The best are drinkable when young and are not too harsh, nor too soft.

Château de la Reynaudie 1978;
Bergerac 1978;
Blanquette de Limoux 1977;
Côtes de Provence 1979.

Côtes du Haut Roussillon VDQS— The Roussillon region is not far from the Pyrenees and the Spanish border.

In the hot climate of the vineyards around the town of Perpignan, the red grapes ripen and almost burn. Many are used to make fortified dessert wine, but some become dry red table wines. The wines have a "hot" spicy flavor and deep red color.

Blanquette de Limoux— Almost every sparkling wine in the world began its history as a "still" white wine, only to become a sparkling wine in an attempt to improve its flavor. Blanquette de Limoux is no exception. It is made from the Clairette grape, which yields simple, uninteresting white wines. Using the *méthode champenoise*, wine makers here have succeeded in making a pleasantly light and dry sparkling wine.

OTHER SOUTHWEST REGIONS

Some of these regions are near Bordeaux, so their wines have characteristics similar to both Bordeaux and Languedoc-Rousillon wines.

Bergerac AC— The town of Bergerac is almost close enough to Bordeaux to qualify as *AC* Bordeaux wine, but in fact it has its own *appellation*. Both red and white wines produced here are light and dry. An exception to this rule is a very special wine called Monbazillac. This rich, sweet wine is made by a traditional method similar to that used for Sauternes. It is only made in good years, and the price per bottle compares favorably with a good Sauterne.

Gaillac AC— Further inland, by the river Tarn, are the Gaillac vineyards. They produce delicate dry and medium-sweet white wines and some sparkling wine. The label of these wines bear the name Gaillac.

Wines of Germany

The three most important items to look for on a German wine label are in this order—the village or vineyard name, the grape variety, and the quality rating of the wine.

German wines are divided into three main categories of quality:

Tafelwein—This is an everyday table wine from any German wine region. It may be a blend of various wines from different vintages.

Qualitätswein—This word means *quality wine*. To get this rating, the wine is tested by a panel of government experts. If approved, the wine bears the letters *QbA*, together with the name of the district of origin.

Qualitätswein mit Pradikat—This rating is for fine wines, and is similar to the French *appellation contrôlée*. Any wine marked *QmP* is tested by specialists each year. If the wine is not top quality due to a bad grape harvest, the tasters downgrade the wine. If the wine is approved, it is further classified according to the way it was made. These additional descriptions also imply sweetness:

Kabinett: A high-quality, special-reserve wine made from fully ripe grapes.

Spätlese: A wine of equal quality to *Kabinett*, but made with grapes picked a little later. This can give a sweeter wine than a *Kabinett* grade.

Auslese: This grade is made from specially selected late-harvest grapes.

Beerenauslese: Sweet wine is made

from grapes picked by hand after they have partially dried on the vine.

Trockenbeerenauslese: Expensive sweet wine made from hand-selected

Neuleininger Hollenpfad, Portugieser
  Rotwein, 1979 QbA;
Johannisberger Erntebringer, Riesling,
  1980 QbA;
Piesporter Michelsberg, 1980 QbA;
Kaiserstuhl-Tuniberg, Müller-Thurgau,
  1977 QbA.

grapes affected by the noble rot *botrytis cinerea,* known in Germany as *edelfäule.*

Eiswein: Literally *ice wine,* this drink is made from grapes that have frozen on the vine.

If the weather in any year is poor and the grapes cannot ripen fully, then no *QmP* wine can be made. By law, grapes that become *QmP* wine must have a minimum sugar concentration. If the grapes are not sweet enough, the wine maker is permitted to add small amounts of cane sugar to the unfermented grape juice to raise the final alcohol level and improve the flavor of the wine. This process is called *verbessert.* He may do this with *Tafelwein* or *QbA* wine, but never with a finished or *QmP* wine.

Main grape varieties used in Germany are white. These include the Riesling, Sylvaner, Müller-Thurgau, Scheurebe, Traminer, and Rulander grapes. One or more of these grapes may be named on the label.

Geographical names on a label of German wines can include the region, district, village and vineyard. You can recognize the village and vineyard names on the label by the *-er* at the end of the village name. The next word indicates the name of the vineyard. For example, if you see *Piesporter Goldtröpfchen,* this means the wine is from the Goldtröpfchen vineyard in Piersport.

OTHER WORDS YOU'LL SEE ON GERMAN LABELS

Echt: Genuine.
Edel: Noble.
Erzeugerabfüllung: Wine bottled by the producer.
Rotwein: Red wine.
Sekt: *QbA* sparkling wine made with the champagne method.
Schaumwein: Non-*QbA* sparkling wine.
Trocken: Dry wine.
Weinkellerei: Wine cellar.
Weisswein: White wine.
Winzergenossenschaft: Grape-grower's cooperative.

RHEINGAU

Famous wines from the Rhine are known as *hock,* after the town of Hochheim, which was the port used for shipping the wine. Rhine wines are almost always bottled in brown glass. The traditional tall slender shape is associated worldwide with German wines.

The Rheingau region is the home of many well-known German wines, including Schloss Johannisberg, the most prestigious of all. It is also the home of German wine technology and education. The national college of enology, or wine science, is in Geisenheim. Research is done there on the use of vine varieties and the effects of soil and climate on grapes. At Kloster Eberbach, special courses on German wines are open to amateurs and professionals.

GRAPE VARIETIES

The region is chiefly planted with the Riesling grape. It makes some flowery, delicate wines that have no equal in the world. Small amounts of Pinot Noir grapes, called *Spätburgunder* in Germany, are grown around the town of Assmannshausen. They yield dry red wine.

Most of the land in this region has been surveyed and tested by the researchers from Geisenheim. The higher slopes, which have chalky soil, have proved best for quality wines from the Riesling grape. Sheltered slopes facing south have less chance of

being ravaged by frost and wind, an important consideration in a cool climate. The word ending *-berg* is German for *mountain*, so it is no coincidence that several of the finest vineyards have the letters in their name, such as in Schloss Johannisberg, Rudesheimer Berg, and Steinberg.

RÜDESHEIM

Many well-known vineyards cluster around this town. The vineyard nearest to the town is world-famous for a pleasant, reliable wine—Rüdesheimer Rosengarten. Better vineyards are on

Hochheimer Daubhaus, Riesling Spätlese, 1976 QmP;
Hochheimer Königin Victoria Berg, Beerenauslese, 1971 QmP;
Schloss Schönborn, Hattenheimer Pfaffenberg, Riesling Beerenauslese, 1971 QmP.

the steep slopes of the Rüdesheimer Berg. Some experts say that the lower vineyards produce better wine when the climate is dry and sunny. As a general rule, however, Berg wines are usually better and more expensive.

JOHANNISBERG

This town is home of the legendary Schloss Johannisberg wine. The word *schloss* means *castle* in German and will be found on German labels. The fruity, and sometimes sweet, wine is so famous that in California some wines made from the Riesling grape are called Johannisberg Riesling in honor of these German Riesling wines.

SCHLOSS VOLLRADS

Almost as renowned as Schloss Johannisberg nearby, Schloss Vollrads is actually in the village of Winkel. The 1971 wine law made Schloss Vollrad a suburb of Winkel, but the name of the wine didn't change. Other wines similar to this one will have the name *Winkeler* on the label, such as Winkeler Hasensprung. Riesling grapes are used.

MITTLEHEIM, HALLGARTEN, OESTRICH, HATTENHEIM

These are well-known and respected villages with many fine vineyards using the Riesling grape. Look for

these names on the label. These wines have been described as "earthy" and "robust."

KIEDRICH AND ERBACH

Erbach is close to the river. Kiedrich is farther away with higher slopes said to give finer wines, notably Kiedricher Grähfenberg. Wines from these towns are full-bodied, elegant drinks.

ELTVILLE

The town of Eltville am Rhein is the center of some aristocratic wine making. Baron von Simmern and the Count Eltz live here and own vineyards in nearby Rauenthal. The wines are considered very fine and bear the names of their noble proprietors on the label. Naturally, this tradition and nobility is reflected in the price of the wines.

Some people call any German Rhine wine a "hock." This is legitimate only for wines from this town. Good wines are made here. The best are from the Domdechaney and Kirchenstück vineyards.

A well-known wine is made from a vineyard named after Queen Victoria, who was partial to hock. This wine is the Hochheimer Königen-Viktoria-Berg.

RHEINPFALZ, NAHE & RHEINHESSEN

Here, wine is made from lovely vineyards on the slopes of the Haardt mountains. These are a continuation of the Vosges, which also shelter Alsace vines. Even so, the wines are not at all similar. Conditions in the Rheinpfalz allow the vines to give high yields. Sometimes, the grapes can ripen fully to give high-quality *Auslese* wines.

The Nahe vineyards lie north of the Rheinpfalz. Wines from this region are grown on the steep banks of the river Nahe, a tributary of the Rhine. Conditions here are not as perfect as those of the Rheinpfalz, but the vine seems to win the battle for existence. These wines have finer flavor than those from vineyards farther south.

Rheinhessen is between the Rheinpfalz and the Nahe. In 1404 the Riesling vine was first given its name here. This is also the home of the legendary Liebfraumilch. According to tradition, this wine comes from the vineyard surrounding Liebfrauenkirche, the Church of Our Lady, at Worms.

Liebfraumilch is now defined as a hock-style wine that comes from the areas of the Rheinhessen, Nahe or Rheinpfalz. It is a wine in the *QbA* category. Because it is blended, vintage dates do not apply

GRAPE VARIETIES

The forested foothills of the Rheinpfalz contain a variety of soils, including rich loam, gravel, chalk, sandstone, and volcanic rock. Different grapes flourish in each type of soil. On the chalky soils, Sylvaner and Müller-Thurgau do well. Both are related to Riesling and give softer versions of fine Riesling wine. Müller-Thurgau is a prolific crossbred grape that is interplanted with Riesling and Sylvaner.

Other grape varieties found here include the spicy Gewürztraminer and related Traminer, the fragrant Morio-Muskat, and the Rulander. Red grapes, such as Portugieser, are also grown.

In the Nahe region, sandstone is the predominant soil. It is a rich, deep red, and lends power to the wine. The main grape varieties of the Nahe are the Riesling, Sylvaner and Müller-Thurgau.

Soil in Rheinhessen is rich and fertile. Grapes grow well. Varieties here include Sylvaner and Müller-Thurgau, which make soft, slightly sweet white wines.

RHEINPFALZ

The Rheinpfalz is Germany's largest wine district. About 15% of the nation's wine is produced here.

Ruppertsberg—In this village in the southern part of the region are the renowned vineyards owned by Dr. Bürklin-Wolf. His wines are much praised and widely available for export. Some quality vineyards to look for are Hoheberg, Goldschmid, and Kreuz.

Deidesheim—The neighboring village of Deidesheim produces both white and rosé wines. The important producers here are Bassermann-Jordan and von Buhl. Look for their names on the label.

Forst—Some of the vineyards here also belong to von Buhl, the largest private vineyard owner in Germany. Vineyard names to look for include Jesuitengarten and Kirchenstuck vineyards. This town makes some of the best wine in Germany and makes much of the *Trockenbeerenauslese*.

Wachenheim—Dr. Bürklin-Wolf also predominates here. The wines are considered very good and full of flavor.

Sausenheimer Honigsack, Hexelrebe Auslese, 1979 QmP;
Niersteiner Gutes Domtal, 1980 QbA;
Schlossböckelheimer Burgweg, Kerner Kabinett, 1977 QmP.

Famous vineyards include Gerümpel, Bödhlig and Goldbächel.

Bad Dürkheim—This town is well known for its sausages, sausage fair, and wines. It is among the top producers of wine in the nation, in terms of output. Its red wines are ordinary, but the whites are rich and full-bodied. The word *Bad* will probably not be on the label of a fine wine.

NAHE

The tributary of the Rhine that winds its way through the mountains gives this town its name. Wines from here can be difficult to find outside of Europe, but your wine dealer may be able to locate some for you.

Bad Kreuznach—This spa town—*bad* means *spa bath*—has some fine vineyards, including the Kausenberg and Oranienberg. Wines made here are fresh and light.

Schloss Böckelheim—Some great German wines are made here in the vineyards of the Kupfergrube. This town is also known as Schlossböckelheim.

Cooperative Wines—Nahe and Rheinpfalz mainly produce fine and expensive wines, but you can also get inexpensive, pleasant wines made by wine cooperatives.

RHEINHESSEN

This district produces wines of higher quality than Liebfraumilch. Some wine makers continue to make wine in the age-old tradition, without mechanization.

Nierstein, Oppenheim and Nackenheim—All three villages have vineyards making flavorful, medium-dry wines. The wines most people know are Niersteiner Gutes Domtal and Oppenheimer Krötenbrunnen. These are inexpensive, everyday wines made in the style of finer wines.

MOSEL-SAAR-RUWER

Some people know this area as Mosel, but due to the 1971 wine laws, the official name of the area for wine labels is Mosel-Saar-Ruwer. Wines made here are light, fruity and charming. Because of the region's climate, the grapes can be more acidic than grapes from other regions. This happens when the grapes do not ripen fully.

The principal river in the area is the picturesque Mosel. The other two rivers, the Saar and Ruwer, are much smaller. Wines from these areas are usually called Mosels too. All Mosel wines are distinguished by their green bottles, instead of the traditional German brown bottle.

GRAPE VARIETIES

The Riesling grape is the most popular type here. Although the climate can be cruel and mean the loss of a whole harvest, in good weather the Riesling matures into a wonderfully flavorful fruit.

For the finest wines, wine lovers choose those made from the slate vineyards of the Middle Mosel. The river banks are very steep and difficult to cultivate, but growers in the region have perfected their craft. They are aided by the slate-like soil, which drains well. It dries rapidly and holds together well. The banks, which are as high as 700 feet, face south and southwest and catch the elusive sun.

MOSEL

Many different wines are made in Mosel, but those listed here are among the best available for export.

Trittenheim—This is a southern Mosel town with some fine vineyards making fresh, zesty wines. Vineyard names to look for include Apotheke and Altärchen.

Piesport—Wine lovers from all over the world know this name. Many wines made here are good and inexpensive. But like some fine white Burgundies, their popularity can make

Bereich Beernkastel, 1978 QbA;
Piesporter Goldtröpfchen, Riesling, 1978 QbA;
Zeller Schwarze Katz 1979;
Trittenheimer Altärchen, Riesling Auslese, 1979 QmP.

their authenticity questionable. Avoid this problem by looking for the name of a vineyard on the label.

Piesporter Michelsberg is a pleasant, inexpensive wine. It is named after a *grosslage*, a group of small vineyards. Another famous wine is Piesporter Goldtröpfchen, which means *drops of gold*. In good years, this is an exquisite wine with a special honey-like flavor.

Bernkastel—This is the general name for a large area of the finest Mosel region. Wines may vary in quality from pleasant and drinkable to rare and expensive. Generally, they are drier than other Mosel wines.

Bereich Bernkastel is a wine that comes from the general area. It is a blended wine, usually low-priced. Bernkasteler Badstube and Bernkasteler Kurfurstlay are *grosslage* names for the product of several vineyards. Some are excellent values. Bernkasteler Doktor is an example of a rare, fine Mosel from a single vineyard.

Graach—Some experts considered the village a top-quality producer. Recommended vineyards include Abtsberg,

Heiligenhaus, Monch and Himmelreich.

Wehlen—Top-quality wines also come from this small village. Look for these vineyards—Abtei, Lay, Sonnenuhr, and Rosenberg.

Zeltingen and Zell—These two areas have a variety of wines—some fine, some ordinary. Most wines from this area are slightly sweet. At Zell the best-known wine is called Schwarze Katz. Look for the black cat on the label.

SAAR

When the weather is good for grapes, this region produces some of the region's finest wines. However, in bad years the wine needs extra sugar or blending to become drinkable.

Ockfen and Ayl—The most exciting wines from this area are Ockfener Bockstein and Ayler Kupp.

RUWER

Good wines from this region are less alcoholic than other Mosels. They are described as lighter and softer.

Kasel—The small vineyards around this village are among the best known in the area. One vineyard is Nieschen.

Maximin Grünhaus—This is the name of the vineyard that produces the wine. The vineyard name is so famous that the village name, Mertesdorf, is not used on the label. Wines from this hidden corner of the Ruwer have a fresh taste that is slightly acidic. Wine-label collectors prize its attractive labels.

BADEN & FRANCONIA

The southern area of Baden and its neighbor Württemberg have extensive vineyards producing consistently good wines. None are of top quality, but most are good enough for everyday drinking.

Franconia lies farther north, not far from Frankfurt, on the river Main. Wines from this region have the reputation of being Germany's most powerful. They have a special "earthy" flavor prized by many wine lovers.

GRAPE VARIETIES

A large variety of grapes flourish on the heat-retaining volcanic soil of Baden. These include full-flavored Rülander (Pinot Gris), spicy Gewürztraminer and Gutedel, which makes light, dry wines. Gutedel is known as Chasselas in France. Spätburgunder (Pinot Noir) is also widely grown and used to make both rosé and red wines.

In Württemberg, a region centered around the city of Stuttgart, a great deal of ordinary red wine is made from the Trollinger grape. Little, if any, is exported. The Spätburgunder and another red grape called Lemberger are also grown. The white wines of the region are of better quality and are made from Traminer and Sylvaner grapes. Many crops in this area around the river Neckar are lost due to early frosts.

Grapes used to make the wine in the Franconia include Müller-Thurgau, Sylvaner and some red-wine varieties. Growing conditions give the wines a dry flavor and subtle finish similar to those in dry French wines.

BADEN

Baden faces the Alsace region of France across the river Rhine. Weather here is pleasantly warm, and the lovely scenery of the Black Forest surrounds the vineyards. Unlike the beer drinkers in the rest of Germany, the locals here drink wine with their meals as the French do. Most Baden wines are consumed in the region, but the situation is changing as more are available for export.

Weissherbst—This is a popular, light-colored rosé, made from Spätburgunder grapes. Most is made in the area around the Bodensee lake, with village names such as Meersburger and Opfinger.

Durbacher Josephsberg, Spätburgunder Rotwein, Trocken, 1977 QbA;
Merdinger Bühl, Spätburgunder Rotwein, Trocken, 1979 QbA;
Opfinger Sonnenberg, Spätburgunder Weissherbst Auslese, 1976 QmP.

Kaiserstuhl—Most of the wine from here is made by a large cooperative. The wine is usually soft and fragrant in style, medium-dry in flavor, and relatively inexpensive.

Ortenau—Some fine wines are made here from the Riesling grape, which in Baden is called the *Klingelberger*. Village names to watch for include Durbach and Neuweier.

FRANCONIA

Wines from the region are easy to recognize because they are sold in a traditional bottle known as a *bocksbeutel*. The green bottle has a special flat shape like a flask.

Steinwein—Some people call all Franconia wines by this name. However, there is also a vineyard called Stein. It is in the area of Würzburg, a beautiful city in the heart of Franconia. Other vineyards here include Schlossberg and Leiste. Wines from this region are generally considered dry for a German wine. In hot years a very sweet *Beerenauslese* is also made.

AHR

This small wine region is close to Bonn, far north of the regions mentioned already. It is a large producer of red wines that tend to be pale in color dué to the harsh climate. Grapes grown include the Spätburgunder and the Portugieser. The Portugieser is a grape yielding everyday red table wine. These wines are rarely exported.

Wines of Italy

Italy was given the name *Oenotria*, Land of Vines, by the Greeks because vines grow abundantly almost everywhere. From the Alps to Sicily, almost every type of wine is made. Italy is the world's largest wine producer, but only since 1960 has a good selection of Italian wines been enjoyed all over the world. Prior to this only a few Italian wines were known outside of Italy.

Most Italian wine is red wine. As in France, wine is an everyday drink in Italy. It is a perfect complement to the fine foods of Italy.

ITALIAN WINE LAWS

The Italian wine-control laws enacted in 1963 are modeled after French *appellation contrôlée* laws and have jurisdiction over the best Italian wines.

Before the introduction of the laws, the quality of Italian wine was extremely variable. There were no rules or regulations concerning wines with particular names. Some producers were making consistently good wine, others decidedly poor wine. Both could have the same name.

The first people to realize that this situation was harmful to business were the producers themselves. They formed regional groups called *consorzio* to impose rules and restraints to control the quality of well-known wines. These growers' groups were organized before the wine laws and are still active today.

The Italian naming system is called *denominazione controllata*. Like the *consorzi's* regulations, it controls the quantity of grapes produced from an acre of vines, the amount of juice ob-

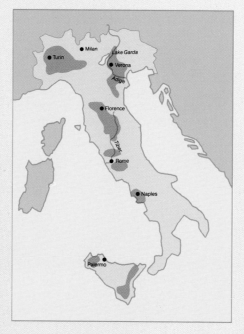

tained from those grapes, and the minimum alcoholic content of the resulting wine.

Italian wine laws have three categories of quality:

Denominazione di Origine Simplice—These are simple Italian wines that are rarely exported. The government can declare the name of the wine, depending on where the grapes were grown. However, there is little government regulation of this type of wine, so there can be no guarantee of quality, as with any ordinary wine.

Barbera 1976;
Soave 1979;
Chianti Ruffino.

Denominazione di Origine Controllata—These "controlled" wines are more regulated than simple ones. To get a *DOC* classification, the wine maker submits his wine to a committee that decides whether the wine is good enough. If it is, the wine maker agrees to conform to the rules mentioned earlier. To date, there are over 200 wines with *DOC* status.

Denominazione di Origine Controllata e Garantita—This classification is reserved for top-quality wines. It is rarely seen, and given only to a few select, expensive wines. More wine makers are trying to get *DCG* status for their wines, but because they are government guaranteed, the wines must truly be the best available.

OTHER WORDS YOU'LL SEE ON ITALIAN LABELS

Amabile: Medium sweet.
Amarone: Bitter.
Bianco: White.
Cantina: Winery or cellar.
Dolce: Very sweet.
Fattoria: A large winery.
Frizzante: Slightly sparkling.
Imbottigliato nel'origine: Estate bottled.
Riserva: Wine aged for at least three years at its place of production.
Rosato: Pink.
Rosso: Red.
Secco: Dry.
Spumante: Sparkling wine.
Stravecchio: Very old.
Vecchio: Old.
Vendemmia: Vintage date.
Vino da Tavola: Table wine.

PIEDMONT & NORTHERN ITALY

If you enter Italy from France through the tunnel below Mont Blanc, the beautiful mountainous area you first encounter is Piedmont. Turin is the big city here, famous for Fiat cars and vermouth, a fortified wine. The best red wine is found south of the city in the towns of Alba, Alessandria and Asti.

East of Piedmont is Lombardy, with the giant industrial city of Milan. Wine is made here too, although industry takes precedence. The best wines have the regional name Valtellina. These are moderately priced.

Farther east is the Austrian border amid the lovely scenery of the South Tyrol. This area has two names—one German, the other Italian. Labels are often bilingual too, and at first glance the lettering on the label looks like German script. However, the wines are distinctively different from those of Germany. Most are pleasantly light, everyday wines. Many are made in cooperatives, so are inexpensive.

GRAPE VARIETIES

The Alps overshadow all of Northern Italy, lending shelter to the vineyards in the foothills. The hot summers are followed by cool weather in autumn and winter. The climate promotes pungent, sweet grapes, resulting in wines with high alcoholic content. In fact, some Barolo wines from Piedmont are 15% alcohol.

Grapes grown in Piedmont include Nebbiolo and Barbera for full-bodied red wines, and Freisa, Dolcetto and Grignolino for lighter red wines.

Lombardy has many wines named for their grape variety, including Barbera, Pinot and Riesling. In the Trentino, the German influence of nearby Austria extends the choice of grapes grown. Most of the white wines are made with Pinot, Riesling and Traminer. The Merlot grape is used to make soft red wines.

PIEDMONT

The great wines of Piedmont are long-lived, powerful red wines. Wine makers recommend that you let these wines breathe for about two hours before drinking. They are among the most expensive Italian wines. Some sweet white and rosé wines are also made here.

Barolo and Barbaresco—These two wines are made with the Nebbiolo grape. Both are named after small villages. Barolo is a special full-bodied red wine used for celebrations and important events. By law it must be aged in wood for over three years. It is often aged even longer before being bottled.

Barbaresco is a lighter wine, aged for a shorter period in a wooden cask. It is less expensive than Barolo.

Barbera—Don't confuse this with the two wines just described. All are dry and red, but there the resemblance ends. This wine is named for the grape used. It is usually fruitier and lighter than Barolos and Barbarescos. You can recognize the best Barberas by looking for the name of the wine-making district after the name *Barbera*. Those labeled *superiore* are at least 13% alcohol.

Gattinara—Experts rate this wine as very fine in years of good harvests. Like Barolo, it is a dry and rich red wine made from the Nebbiolo grape. It is named after the town of origin. The best Gattinaras are called Spanna Gattinara and have at least 12% alcohol.

Nebbiolo—This is a simple table wine named for the grape. It can be made from blends of excess production from a good vineyard. It is a good buy.

LOMBARDY

The best wines here are produced from grapes grown on steeply terraced slopes. As in Piedmont, the red wines are made with the Nebbiolo grape.

Valtellina—The *DOC* uses this name for strong red wines made from vines cultivated on the steep banks of the river Adda. The most important red wines are called Inferno, Sassella and Grumello.

Lugana—The Trebbiano grape goes into this full-bodied white wine. It is one of the few white wines aged in wooden casks.

Frecciarossa—The vineyards of this village belong to one family, in the tradition of French estates. Many wines are available. They include a white wine, La Vigne Blanche, made with the Riesling grape, a rosé named Pinot Nero, and a medium-sweet white wine. Even though they have French names, in addition to *Frecciorossa* on the label, they are distinctively Italian.

Trentino—Many wines here are simple, everyday red wines named for their grape varieties, as in Cabernet Trentino and Merlot Trentino.

Santa Maddalena—Schiava and Lagrein grapes become this full-bodied red wine. Lagrein is also used to make a deep pink rosé that is popular in Switzerland.

Asti Spumante;
Barolo;
Nebiolo.

TUSCANY & UMBRIA

Tuscany is well known for Chianti, Italy's most famous red wine. Part of its appeal is due to the attractive presentation of the bottle in a straw-covered flask, called a *fiasco*. This type of packaging was developed to protect the bottle from breakage, when glass was expensive. Today this practice is less common because the cost of making the special bottles is becoming prohibitive.

However, the wines are better than ever. Many Chiantis are now sold under the name of the estate owner, in the same way as French claret is sold under the name of the château. The major Chianti area is known as Chianti Classico. These wines have a distinctive black rooster on the seal to indicate the wine maker's membership in the local *consorzio*. Others from outlying areas belong to another *consorzio*, Chianti Putto, which has a cherub on the neck of the bottle as its motif.

There are other fine red and white wines from this region of central Italy.

GRAPE VARIETIES

On the Tuscan hills between Florence and Siena, the earth is dry and sandy. Vines intermingle with olive trees. The grapes that become Chianti include Sangiovese, a delicately flavored red variety, and a white variety, Malvasia. The blend for each producer is a secret. Other grapes that may be

Chianti Ruffino;
Orvieto;
Chianti Spalletti.

used are the Cannaiolo and the Trebbiano. Some grapes may come from the warm areas of Southern Italy.

The medieval city of Orvieto in Umbria stands high on an outcrop of volcanic rock. This is said to give a special dry, almost bitter flavor to the white wine made with Trebbiano grapes. The wine matures in caves deep in the rock.

TUSCANY

Wines from the Tuscan hillsides can generally be described as full-bodied and rich. These are some of Italy's most consistent red wines.

Chianti—You'll find this famous wine in two different styles. The young, less expensive wine resembles Beaujolais. It is fruity, delicious and best consumed young. After the young wine has completed fermentation, some wine makers add a little juice taken from the pressing of sun-dried grapes. This sweet addition causes a secondary fermentation, which puts some carbon dioxide gas in the wine for a slight sparkle.

The finest Chianti is aged for several years in oak casks. This is always sold in claret-style bottles. It is labeled *Riserva* and has a subtle flavor and orange tint. It is more expensive than most Chianti but is worth the difference.

Some Chiantis bottled on private estates are Vicchiomaggio, Ricasoli, Antinori and Frescobaldi.

Vernaccia di San Gimignano—This dry white wine is made from the Vernaccia grape. Its fine taste improves after a couple of years of aging in the bottle.

Brunello di Montalcino and Vino Nobile de Montepulciano—Both wines are made with Brunello grape, related to the Sangiovese grape used for Chianti. Aged in the cask for five to six years, these wines have a powerful, full-bodied flavor like some fine Rhône wines.

UMBRIA

South of Tuscany is the central region of Umbria. Here some good-quality red and white wines are made.

Orvieto—You'll find two styles of this excellent white wine. If the wine is labeled *abboccato* or *amabile*, it is medium-sweet. This is considered the old style of Orvieto. Due to the popularity of dry wines, dry Orvieto, labeled *secco,* is also made.

Torgiano—Not far from Assisi, birthplace of St. Francis, is the Torgiano district. You can find pleasant red and white wines here.

VERONA & EASTERN ITALY

From the area surrounding Verona come some of Italy's most popular wines, including Valpolicella, Soave and Bardolino. Not far from the city of Verona is the lovely city of Venice, with its inland waterways and many little *trattorias* serving these wines.

Down the coast from Verona and Lake Garda is the region called Emilia-Romagna. The major city here is Bologna, known more for its rich and delicious food than for wine. However, some very pleasant wines are made here, including the unusual red sparkling Lambrusco.

Farther south is the Marches, hilly country with simple ordinary wines. One known throughout the world is Verdicchio dei Castelli di Jesi, a refreshingly dry white wine often sold in elaborate and decorative bottles.

GRAPE VARIETIES

The gentle hills of Verona are fortunate to have an excellent climate and stony soil that drains well. Both are ideal for vine cultivation. Dry white Soave wines are made from the Garganega and Trebbiano grapes.

Valpolicella and Bardolino are dry red wines made with Corvina Veronese and Rondinella grapes. Both are local varieties.

In Emilia-Romagna the landscape is rich and fertile. This is not ideal for grape vines, which seem to prefer to struggle for existence. The Lambrusco is named after the local grape from which it is made.

Mountains of the Marches are windy and sometimes harsh to the vines growing there. The white grapes grown here are Verdicchio, Trebbiano and Malvasia.

VERONA

This is one of Italy's largest wine-producing regions, second only to Apulia in the South.

Soave 1979;
Lambrusco Amabile;
Verdicchio dei Castelli di Jesi;
Valpolicella 1977 in wine basket.

Soave—The *DOC* district for this white wine is about 15 miles from Verona, near the village of Soave. There are two different styles of Soave. One is familiar to wine lovers in many countries as a dry, Chablis-like wine.

The other is Recioto di Soave, a wine made with grapes dried by the sun before pressing. The resulting wine is sweet and has a high alcoholic content, with an aftertaste that is compared to bitter almonds. The wine is highly prized in Italy.

Valpolicella—Like Soave, this dry red wine is made two ways. The young, fresh wine should be consumed when very young, within three years after the harvest. Try it slightly chilled.

The Recioto della Valpolicella is slightly sweet for an Italian red wine. If allowed to ferment completely to a dry style, this Valpolicella is known as an *amarone*, a bitter wine. Up to 15% of grapes from outside the *DOC* area may be blended with Valpolicella.

Bardolino—Grapes for Bardolino grow on the southeastern shores of Lake Garda. Up to four different grapes may be blended to make this light, dry wine. It has an attractive pale color, known as *chiaretto* in Italy. Some people prefer this red wine slightly chilled.

EMILIA ROMAGNA

This region is better known for its food than wines. The good wines mentioned here are excellent accompaniments to Northern-Italian dishes.

Albana di Romagna—The Albana grape is used exclusively in this pleasant dry or medium-sweet white wine.

Sangiovese di Romagna—This wine is named after the Sangiovese grape. It is a light, dry red wine becoming popular outside of Italy.

Lambrusco—Rich pork dishes of the region go well with this slightly sparkling, dry red wine. Some people claim it helps digestion.

MARCHES

This region is on the east coast of Italy, next to the Adriatic Sea.

Verdicchio dei Castelli di Jesi—The long and elaborate name refers to the castle where the wine is made. It is a crisp, dry white wine that is ideal with seafood. In fact, you can sometimes find it in a fish-shaped bottle. It may also be labeled just *Verdicchio*.

ROME & SOUTHERN ITALY

The warm southern climate of Italy does not produce the nation's best wines. Even so, there are many delightful everyday wines south of Tuscany. One is Frascati, a dry white wine made in the area around Rome.

Farther south down the western coast is Campania, best known as the Naples holiday region. Wines from this part of Italy are not exciting. The best are sweet.

East of Campania is Apulia, the Central Valley of Italy. It is rich in vineyards, with many hours of sunshine that can scorch the grapes. Soil here tends to be heavy with much clay, giving a coarse flavor to the wines. Many are used for blending with finer northern wines, such as Chianti.

The "toe" of Italy is Calabria, a wild and primitive area with wines to match. The island of Sicily, Italy's "football," has some reliable, everyday wines, notably Corvo in both red and white versions.

GRAPE VARIETIES

The Bolsena district near the lake of the same name and the Alban hills above Rome are good grape-growing areas. The soil is volcanic and is said to give a special fragrance to the wines. Grapes used for white wines include Malvasia Bianca, Trebbiano and Greco.

The hot areas of the south grow many varieties of grapes. The grapes are mainly from the muscat family. They have a distinctively sweet aroma and taste. Some are used for sweet, fortified dessert wines. In Campania, a popular wine for export is Lacrima Christi, made from Greco grapes and others.

LAZIO

This is the province that includes the capital city, Rome.

Est! Est! Est!—This wine is better known for its name than its taste. Legend says that the servant for an 11th century bishop traveling to Rome preceded his master to inspect inns along the way. The bishop instructed his servant to chalk *est*, meaning "Here it is," on the doors of good inns. The servant was so impressed with the wine he tasted at Montefiascone that he wrote *Est! Est! Est!* on the door of the inn.

To this day a light white wine is made with the name. Sometimes it is slightly sparkling, or *frizzante*. It is not widely available outside Italy.

Frascati—Most Frascati found abroad is dry, light and golden. But another style is much sweeter. It is made from grapes affected by noble rot, called *marciume nobile* in Italian. Both are among Italy's finest white wines.

CAMPANIA

This region is on the southwestern coast of Italy and includes Mt. Vesuvius and the city of Naples.

Lacrima Christi—This is a traditional name, meaning *tears of Christ*, that is used for a variety of wines. The true style is a white wine that is slightly sweet and soft, with an alcoholic content between 12 and 13%.

Capri—The island of Capri is famous for its beauty, not its wines. The dry white wine made from the Greco grape is much better than the red made here.

APULIA

This small, sun-soaked region is in southeastern Italy on the coast of the Adriatic. The principal city is Bari.

Primitivo—The full red wines made with this grape are of particular interest to those who know the Zinfandel wines of California. Scientists at the

Frascati 1979;
Lacrima Christi;
Corvo Duca di Salaparuta
white 1975 and red
1979.

University of Davis in California now claim that this is the original Zinfandel grape that was imported to California from Europe in the 19th century.

In Italy it yields a powerful wine that can be excellent in years of good harvest. Like the Zinfandel grape of the hot Central Valley of California, it does well in the hot climate of Apulia. The wine said to resemble Zinfandel most is the Primitivo di Gioia.

SICILY

Sicily is best known as the home of Marsala, a strong, sweet fortified wine. However, Sicily also produces red and white wines.

Capo Bianco and Capo Rosso—These are light white and red wines made in the northeastern part of Sicily. Grapes used include the Chasselas for the white wine and some Barbera for the red. The high alcoholic content of these wines may mask the flavor.

Corvo Bianco, Corvo Rosso—Palermo wineries in the northwestern region produce these. The red wine is better than the white because the climate is too hot for proper cultivation of white grapes. Alcoholic content can be as high as 14.5%.

Etna Bianco, Etna Rosso—As the name suggests, these wines are made from vines grown on the fertile volcanic slopes of Mount Etna. The dry white wines are light in flavor and sometimes *frizzante*. The red may also lack flavor, but some are pleasant this way. Much of this wine goes abroad or to the north for blending.

Wines of Other European Countries

As fine wines from France, Italy and Germany become more expensive, those from lesser-known regions gain popularity. Vineyards have existed for many centuries in most of the regions described here. In some cases, such as the rare sweet Tokay wine of Hungary, the wines were once better known than they are now. Although tastes may change, the good wines remain as good as ever.

Vineyards stretch eastward from Alsace in France in an almost continuous line all the way to the Black Sea. Starting in Switzerland, where light white wines are made amid the Alps, the next wine-making country is Austria, home of fragrant, German-style white wines.

Hungary and Yugoslavia are fast-growing producers of inexpensive, pleasant table wines. And, they have some top-quality wines too. Wine is also made to the north in the Soviet Union, but little is exported.

To the east, the countries that produce wine are Romania and Bulgaria. More Bulgarian than Romanian wine is exported, but in both countries the wine industry is new and still developing.

South of Bulgaria lies Greece, whose wine-making traditions date back to ancient times. Cyprus, the attractive island off the Turkish coast, has long supplied sherry-style wine to the world. It also makes pleasant, ordinary table wine.

No wine tour of Europe could be complete, however, without a good look at Spain and Portugal. Both are blessed with excellent climates and terrains for growing grapes. Their wines are available worldwide. Once wine drinkers thought of this corner of Europe as the home of only sherry and port, but now its table wines are growing in international importance.

Hungarian Olasz Riesling:
Portuguese Dao 1974;
Greek Minos Rosé 1977;
Spanish Vina Sol 1977;
English Biddenden Müller-Thurgau 1979;
Swiss Dôle Valeria 1979.

Much of the inexpensive table wine of Spain and Portugal is exported to France and Italy for use in vermouths and in blends for *vin ordinaire* and *vino da pasto.*

OTHER WORDS YOU'LL SEE ON SPANISH AND PORTUGUESE WINE LABELS*

Anejo, Velho: Old.
Bodega, Adega: Company that makes and ships wine.
Blanco, Branco: White wine.
Brut, Bruto: Dry sparkling wine.
Cepa: Grape variety.
Clarete: Light red wine.
Conseja Regulador: Controlling body administering wine laws.
Cosecha, Colheita: Vintage date.
Dulce, Doce: Sweet wine.
Embotellado, Engarrafado: Bottled.
Espumoso, Espumante: Sparkling wine.
Garrafeira: Date of bottling.
Reserva: Mature quality wine.
Rosado: Rose wine.
Seco: Dry wine.
Tinto: Full-bodied red wine.
Vendemia: Vintage.
Vino de mesa, Vinho de mesa: Ordinary table wine.

* Other European countries translate key words on their wine labels.

SPAIN

Not many years ago, Spain was known to many wine drinkers as the source of sherry and inexpensive table wines. Today the picture is different. Top-quality wines from Rioja and Panadés are impressing connoisseurs everywhere. Spain's wine industry is making tremendous efforts to keep up with modern demands.

SPANISH WINE LAWS

Spain has realized the value of control. The Spanish *Denominación* de Origen is roughly equivalent to the French *appellation contrôlée* and the Italian *DOC*.

Areas selected for this status include the Navarra and Rioja regions of the north, where the finest red wines of Spain are made. Rioja wines are aged in wood for several years before being bottled. Even the youngest must spend at least two years in oak casks to qualify for the *Denominación de Origen*.

GRAPE VARIETIES

Grapes grow almost everywhere in Spain. Most prevalent in the stony, mountainous northern regions of Navarra and Rioja are the red Garnacho grape, related to the Grenache of southern France, and the red Graciano, a native grape. White wines of this area are made from the Malvasia and Viura grapes.

To the east of the Navarra vineyards are those of Panadés in Catalonia. Thanks largely to the efforts of one producer, wines from this region are now widely recognized as equally good to those of the Rioja. The grapes used are much the same. Very good sparkling wines from this area, made with the *méthode champenoise*.

The other principal wine region of Spain is La Mancha. Grapes used are Cencibal, Monastrel and Tintorera for red wines and Lairen for white wines.

RIOJA

One of the reasons this region produces such good wine is that many French wine makers came here when their vines were destroyed by the vine louse in the late 19th century. Many of these wine makers eventually left, but they left behind expertise.

This region has many *bodegas* making good dry red wines. These are aged in wooden casks before being bottled. To determine the age of a Rioja wine, look at the date on the label. If it is a particular year, such as 1976, then the wine is mainly from that year and possibly "topped up" with a little wine from another vintage. If it says 4 *año* or 5 *año*, the wine aged in casks for four or five years and then bottled.

Marqués de Murrieta 1978;
Imperial 1970;
Marqués de Riscal 1978;
Federico Paternina 1976.

The style of good red Rioja is similar to a French claret. It is rich, dry, and full-bodied. White Rioja resembles white French Burgundy in flavor, due to the aging of the wine in wooden casks. This gives them a special butter-like flavor.

Some shippers to look for on labels of good Rioja include Marqués de Riscal, Marqués de Murrietta, Federico Paternina, Bodegas Riojanas, Bodegas Bilbainas and Bodegas Olarra.

CASTILE

The best-known wine of this region is Vega Sicilia. Although it has an Italian-sounding name, it is definitely Spanish. Wines are aged for a minimum of 10 years before being bottled at the bodega near the town of Penafiel. The result is a full-bodied dry red wine with a complex flavor.

CATALONIA

This region on the coast of the Mediterranean Sea includes the city of Barcelona.

Perelada—Pleasant red and white wines are made here. In addition, it makes some good sparkling wine with the *bulk* process. This is letting the secondary fermentation occur in a vat instead of the bottle.

Tarragona—A selection of wines is made here, including wine-based liqueurs and vermouths. The local wines are used to make bottled *sangria*, a red wine mixed with citrus juices.

Priorato—This town is mainly known for the dark-red wines that are exceptionally strong and powerful.

Panadés—The Torres family owns this area's best bodega and has an international reputation for quality. Their Vina Sol white wine is excellent, as is their Gran Coronas red wine.

San Sadurni de Noya—The town is the center for quality sparkling wines, including those labelled Codorníu and Freixenet.

LA MANCHA

The vast fertile plain made famous by Cervantes' novel *Don Quixote* is a wine-producing area. Most of the wines produced here go to France and Germany for blending.

Valdepenas—Red and white table wines produced here bear the name of the town. Some are good "jug" wines.

PORTUGAL

On Portuguese wine lists there is a distinction between two basic styles of table wine—*vinho verde* (green wine) and *vinho maduro* (mature wine). *Vinho verde* is a young, fresh style that accounts for about 25% of the country's production. *Vinho maduro* is wine aged in casks, including wine from the Dão region and Mateus Rosé. The best-known wine outside Portugal is certainly Mateus Rosé, but in fact a variety of wines in all styles and prices are made here.

The Portuguese *selo de origem* classification is similar to the French *appellation contrôlée* but does not include all regions of the country.

GRAPE VARIETIES

All good Portuguese table wines are made from grapes grown in the north of the country. So are the grapes that become port, a famous fortified wine. The *vinho verde* area is close to the Douro port, in the province of Minho. Here, grapes are grown up trees or on trellises around the edges of fields. Picking the grapes just before full ripeness gives the wine a fresh "green" flavor.

Grapes for red *vinho verde*—the major part of the wine production—are Amaral. Alvarinho and Azal are used for white wine.

In the hilly Dão country many different grape types are grown. These varieties include Tourigo, Tinta Pinheira and Preto Mortagua. They are blended to make distinctive wines.

Not far from Lisbon is a small area

Dão 1974;
Vinho Verde;
Mateus Rosé.

with sandy soil over clay. Ramisco grape vines here are resistant to the vine louse that destroyed the vines of Europe in the 19th century. These few vineyards survived and still make fine red wine today.

OPORTO

This city has given its name to port, a fortified wine for which Portugal is famous. It is widely imitated all over the world, but most connoisseurs agree that the best is from Portugal.

Mateus Rosé—This carbonated rosé wine is very popular. Its short fermentation period is stopped early to allow some sugar to remain in the wine. Then carbon dioxide is added artificially. The result is a pale dry, red wine that tastes best well chilled. It has been described as a wine for people who don't usually drink wines.

Vinho Verde—Most of the exported everyday table wines are white. These wines can be a surprise when first tried. They are acidic and "prickle" your tongue. This is due to a secondary fermentation in the bottle.

DÃO

The Dão—pronounced "dow"—region of central Portugal takes its name from the Dão river. The Mondego and several other streams are close by. Red Dão wines are often aged in wood. Some are compared with French Burgundies. They have a velvety quality and full, rich flavor. The best red wines are selected for longer aging and labeled *Reserva*. White wines are very dry and "flinty," like a Chablis.

Many Dão wines are made by large cooperatives. There are very few named estates or vineyards. One well-known brand called Grao Vasco is made by a large winery called Sogrape. Another is Terras Altas.

LISBON

Vineyards surrounding Portugal's capital city are among the best in the country.

Colares—Grapes used in this rare red wine are grown on sand dunes near the Atlantic ocean. The wine is difficult to find outside of Portugal.

Estramadura—Wines made in this region are the white wines of Torres Vedras, a famous town where Wellington built fortifications to keep out Napoleon. They are not particularly interesting and rarely exported.

Bucelas—This is an unusual dry white wine made from the Arinto grape, with a flavor like Riesling. It is made mainly by Caves Velhas, which also makes Dão wines.

AUSTRIA & SWITZERLAND

Most people don't associate these beautiful alpine countries with wine. In fact, both produce large quantities of well-made white wine. Much is consumed within the country of origin. The strength of the Swiss currency is another reason why Swiss wines are exported only in tiny amounts.

Austrian wine is more available worldwide, due in part to the introduction of wine laws similar to those of Germany. There is a family resemblance between the wines of Austria and Germany. They are graded as *Qualitätswein* and *Qualitätswein mit Pradikat* with the same levels of sweetness—*Kabinett, Spätlese, Auslese, Beerenauslese* and *Trockenbeerenauslese*. Austrian wines in these last two categories of rare sweet wines can be very good values.

GRAPE VARIETIES

The great majority of Austrian wine is white. A little red wine is made with the Pinot Noir and Gamay grapes, but almost never exported. Most Austrian vineyards are in a 50-mile radius around Vienna. Much of the fresh, light dry wine made from the Grüner Veltliner grape is consumed directly from the cask in the taverns and inns of Vienna. Other white grape varieties regularly planted include Riesling, Gewürztraminer, Sylvaner and Müller-Thurgau.

Near the town of Krems on the Danube are the Wachau vineyards. Vines are grown on the north bank of the river, with steep terraces on the rocky soil. Below is the Kamp valley with rich *loess* soil, where lesser quality grapes for blended wine are grown.

Vineyards are scattered all over Switzerland. Some dry red wine is made in the Alpine region bordering Italy. Grapes used are the Merlot, Pinot Noir and Gamay.

As in the French vineyards farther south, vines in the Valais region tumble down the steep banks of the river in dry and sunny conditions. The temperatures are not as high, so white grapes are more successful. The most prevalent grapes grown are the Chasselas grapes—known in Switzerland as the Fendant or Dorin.

AUSTRIA

Generally, Austrian wines have a fuller flavor than those found in top-quality German wines.

Wachau—One well-known independent grower is Lenz Moser, named after the man who pioneered a special system of training vines to grow to a greater height than usual. This gives a high-yield vine with lower labor costs. Wines bearing his name are reliable and fruity. The best-known abroad is Schluck, a brand of wine made from Sylvaner and other grapes.

Vienna—Vineyards surround the capital city. New wine is served in taverns as *heurige*, still slightly sparkling. To the south the vineyards follow the railway toward Hungary. Its most famous village is Gumpoldskirchen, en route to the spa of Baden, a haunt of Mozart and Beethoven. Wine from this village is considered one of Austria's finest, and in good years some sweet, late-harvest wines are made. Another famous wine name in this area is that of Klosterneuburg, home of a wine school.

Austrian Schluk;
Swiss Dôle Valeria 1979 and Johannisberg St. Urbain 1979.

Burgenland—Around Lake Neusied, which juts into Hungary, are vineyards producing excellent sweet, late-harvest wines. The village name to look for is Rust, whose wines have been compared with the legendary Tokay from Hungary.

Weinviertel—The city's name means *wine quarter.* It extends to the Czech border and is planted with Grüner Veltliner grapes, which give a white wine.

SWITZERLAND

This nation borders Germany, France and Italy, producers of some of the world's best wines. Therefore, it is no surprise that the Swiss also produce some fine wines. Their wines are labeled with geographical names, like French wines.

Valais—White wines from this area are made either with the Fendant grape, which gives a dry, slightly bubbly wine or with Sylvaner and Riesling grapes, making a wine usually labelled Johannisberger.

Red wines are called Dôle. They are dry and soft like a light Burgundy. Burgundy is very popular in Switzerland.

Vaud—Red wines here, by Lake Geneva, are called Salvagnin. White wine is made with the Fendant grape, here called Vaud Dorin.

Neuchâtel—North of the Valais and Vaud, toward Bern, are the Neuchâtel vineyards. Wines bear the name of the town and are mainly white, similar in style to the Fendant and Dorin. Sparkling wine is also made here. The delicate and light red wines are made from Pinot Noir grapes. A pale rosé, which looks almost gray, is called *Oeil de Perdrix,* meaning Eye of the Partridge.

YUGOSLAVIA & HUNGARY

Although Hungary and Yugoslavia border each other, there are not many similarities among their wines. Yugoslavia's vineyards stretch over a vast area. The best are in the northeast, in the province of Slovenia. Both Hungary and Yugoslavia are best known abroad for their white wines, but the fiery, powerful red wine, Hungarian Bull's Blood, is also becoming widely available.

GRAPE VARIETIES

The Slovenia province of Yugoslavia has vineyards in the shadow of the Alps. The principal white grape variety here is the Riesling. This is not the noble German grape, but a more humble Italian version that yields pleasant and soft medium-dry wine. Sylvaner is also grown here.

Croatia, south of Slovenia, and Serbia to the southwest, are also wine producers. Some of the grapes grown here include Riesling, Ottonel and Traminac (Traminer) for white wine, and Cabernet for red.

On the limestone coast and rocky islands of Dalmatia is some of Yugoslavia's most lovely scenery and also many vineyards. The alcoholic and powerful wine made here reflects the intensity of the summers. Grape varieties include Plavac and Opol for red

Yugoslavian Lutomer Laski Riesling and Malena Traminer;
Hungarian Bull's Blood (Egri Bikavér, and Tokaji Aszu.

wines, and Marastina for white wines.

The majority of Hungary's wine is grown on the sandy plains of the Danube River. Most is ordinary table wine made from red Kadarka and white Riesling grapes. As you move north toward the Soviet Union, the next wine region is around Eger in the volcanic hills of Matra. The most famous wine made here is red Bull's Blood.

Northeast of here are the Tokay hills, home of a very special golden wine named Tokay. This has inspired many imitators all over the world, but none have been truly successful. The finest Tokay is affected by the noble rot *botrytis cinerea* which also affects the grapes made into French Sauternes. It is sweet and has a powerful flavor. The white grapes used to make Tokay are Furmint and Hárslevelü.

Another important Hungarian wine region is at Lake Balaton, an attractive resort area. Vines flourish on the hills around the lake on sandy soil with some volcanic outcrops. The sun on the lake is reflected back on to the vines, promoting additional ripeness. The white wines are made with the Riesling—known as the Olasz Riesling in Hungary. Furmint is also grown here.

YUGOSLAVIA

Wines exported from Yugoslavia are usually labeled with the grape variety and the district that produced the wine. Cooperatives make most of this exported wine.

Slovenia—The region's most famous export is called Lutomer Riesling, a light, blended wine made with the Italian Riesling grape.

Another well-known name is Tiger Milk, a *Spätlese* wine from the Ranina estate near the town of Radgona.

Dalmatia—The range of wines here is almost as varied as the islands off the coast. An oddly named red wine, Grk, is famed for its strength. A dry white called Zilavka is also good.

HUNGARY

Hungarian wine is exported by the state monopoly called *Monimpex*.

Tokay—The vineyards around the town of Tokay grow the Furmint and Hárslevelü grapes. These sometimes develop the noble rot *botrytis cinerea*. In Hungary, such grapes are known as *aszu* and are used to make a sweet wine like the German *Auslese*. They are crushed in tubs called *puttonyos*. The wine made from them is blended with "ordinary" wine made from grapes unaffected by the rot.

On a label of the wine, called Tokaji Aszu, you'll see a rating of three, four or five *putton(y)os*. This indicates the proportion of sweet, noble-rot wine used in the blend. The rarest and sweetest is five *putton(y)os*, made with 100% *botrytis* grapes. This is the wine that the Czars of Russia thought had magic powers. It was sometimes aged for 200 years before drinking. Even today it is one of the world's longest-lived wines.

A dry style of Tokay, called Tokaji Szamorodni, is also made.

Eger—Between Tokay and Budapest is the old town of Eger, home of Bull's Blood, a heavy red wine made from the Kadarka grape. It may also be called Egri Bekavér. Look for a bull's head on the label.

Balaton—The region includes Lake Balaton, the largest lake in Europe. Inexpensive white wines made with Riesling and Furmint grapes predominate here.

Mir—Míri Ezerjí is a typical dry Hungarian white wine. It has a golden color and the flavor of honey.

Sopron—This is the Hungarian part of the Burgenland, where fresh, young red wine called Soproni Kékfrankos is made.

GREECE & CYPRUS

Because the climate is hot here, the wines are usually made in sweet styles. The best are rich and liqueur-like. Both countries have centuries-old wine-making traditions. Until recently the methods used were identical to those of the Ancient Greeks. However, the past 20 years have brought many modern improvements in wine-making technology.

The wine for which Greece is most famous is retsina, a white wine flavored with pine resin. Both Greece and Cyprus make ordinary table wine too. Today, its quality is improving and more is being exported.

One problem in choosing a wine from this area is the lettering on the label. Fortunately there are some brand names that help you to identify the style of wine in spite of the label's script.

GRAPE VARIETIES

Greece produces about as much wine as the Bordeaux region of France. A third of her vineyards are in the Peloponnese, the peninsula southwest of Athens. Much sweet wine is made here with Malvasia grapes.

The historic island of Crete has some good wines made from vines that did not succumb to the vine louse *phylloxera* in the 19th century. Red wines here are made with the Kotsifali grape.

Naoussa in Northern Greece has a relatively cool climate for Greece. These are vineyards on the slopes of Mount Velia. The best red wines are made with the Xynomavro, which makes flavorful *mavro* (black) wines.

The main grape varieties grown in Cyprus are the red Mavron, white Xynisteri and red Muscat of Alexandria.

GREECE

The best Greek wines have a government seal over the neck of the bottle.

Peloponnese—Nemea, a red wine called "the blood of Hercules," is a dry, full-bodied local wine. Mantinia is a dry white wine. Near the town of Patras, rich dessert wines are made from the red Mavrodaphne grape. There is also a sweet Muscat of Patras.

Crete—Two red wines considered good examples of Cretan winemaking are Archanes and Peza. Daphne's sweet wine from the hill country of Crete was known in medieval England as Malmsey. The island also produces a strong rosé. One of the popular brands is Minos.

Demestica—Wine makers use this brand name for a reliable table wine, made in both red and white styles.

Retsina—Centuries of tradition go into this wine. It is a pine-scented drink made by adding pine resin to dry white wine. Originally, this was

Cyprian Aphrodite and Othello; Greek Minos Rosé 1977, Corinth Retsina and Demestica.

done in ancient times to help preserve the wine. It has a curiously sharp flavor similar to turpentine. Some people say it goes well with oily Greek food.

CYPRUS

Cyprus is famous for sweet red wine, made from grapes grown in the Troodos Mountains. The 19th century vine louse did not affect Cyprus, which has *phylloxera*-free vineyards to this day.

Commanderia—Traditionally, this was a sweet wine made from the concentrated juice of sun-dried grapes, both red and white. Today it is a commercial dessert wine without any special characteristics. Only a very few wineries still make it in the traditional manner, resulting in a wine four times sweeter than port. Many people dilute it with water before drinking it.

Platres—Red wine and some rosé is made in this region. Kokkineli is one brand of rosé.

Paphos—White wine is made here. Pitsilla is the best-known wine.

Keo, Sodap and Haggipavlu—These are large firms that ship most Cyprian table wine. Some brand names to look for include Othello for red wine and Arsinoe and Aphrodite for white wine. All are inexpensive blended wines.

SOVIET UNION, ROMANIA, BULGARIA & ENGLAND

There are more wine drinkers in these countries than most people realize. Although vodka is the national drink of Russia, wine is also consumed with meals. In addition to producing large quantities of wine, the Soviet Union also imports wine from Romania and Bulgaria.

Romania has the same latitude as France, so some experts think Romania has the potential to make French-style wines. Bulgarian wines are inexpensive, and like Soviet Union and Romanian wines, controlled by a State Wine Board. The flavor and style of some can be compared to some of the good wines of Western Europe.

GRAPE VARIETIES

Vineyards spread across southern Russia, growing grapes of all kinds. Many are traditional varieties, but now some finer types such as Riesling and Cabernet, are grown. Sweet sparkling wines are very popular. The Crimean peninsula and the Republic of Georgia are said to produce the best wines. Few are exported to non-Communist countries.

Romania is known mainly for white wines. Moldavia in the northeast is the home of a sweet wine in the Tokay style. Western grapes include Riesling, Aligoté and Pinot. Chardonnay does well in Murfatlar, near the Bulgarian border.

Bulgaria grows Cabernet and Chardonnay grapes for good red and white wines. Riesling also grows successfully here.

SOVIET UNION

Ukraine—This republic has the largest vineyards in the Soviet Union. Red, white and sparkling wines are made here, as well as a dessert wine called Massandra. It is made from muscat grapes.

Georgia—Dry white wines include Tsinandali and Gurdzhaan. Mukuzani and Saperavi are red wines of lesser quality.

ROMANIA

You may not be able to find Romanian wine because most of what is exported goes to other Communist countries.

Cotnari—Many people compare this once-famous sweet dessert wine with Hungarian Tokay. It is made in Moldavia.

Transylvania—A light Riesling wine and the slightly sweet Perla are made here.

Romanian Banat Riesling and Cabernet Sauvignon;
Bulgarian Balkan Vine Pinot Chardonnay and Cabernet Sauvignon;
English Biddenden Müller-Thurgau 1979 and Flexerne 1979.

Murfatlar—Some sweet muscat wine and Chardonnay is made here.

BULGARIA

Much of Bulgaria's wine-making facilities and vines are less that 40 years old. Most of the industry was rebuilt after of World War II.

Black Sea Coast—The country's best dry white wines are from this region

Karvolo—The muscat grape is made into a wine called Misket. It is made into a dry red wine in the style of an Alsatian wine.

Vinimpex—This is the state monopoly that exports wines. These include red Mavrud and Gamza; Hemus, a medium-sweet white; Tamianka, a very sweet white; and the sparkling wine Iskra.

ENGLAND

The climate in England is cool for grapes, and varieties must be carefully selected to ensure that grapes will ripen. This is why most vineyards are in the south of England. Even so, the crop is often lost or much depleted due to bad weather and attacks by birds and squirrels.

White wines are far more successful here than red wines. A small amount of red wine is made from the Pinot Noir grape but, as in Germany, the northerly climate means a loss of color and flavor in red wines.

For white wines, a German style prevails. It is fresh, acidic and fruity. Grape varieties include Müller-Thurgau, Seyval Blanc, and several other German varieties. In most years the wine needs the addition of extra sugar in the grape juice to raise the alcohol content of the fermenting wine.

Beaulieu—These vineyards in Hampshire were originally planted by Cistercian monks in the Middle Ages. Today they produce white wine and some rosé.

Hambledon—This Hampshire vineyard is owned by Sir Guy Salisbury-Jones. The label's motif comes from the first cricket club that was at Hambledon.

Adgestone—Wines grown at this vineyard benefit from the mild climate of the Isle of Wight off the south coast of England.

Felstar—The wine made at this vineyard was among the first English wines to gain the English equivalent of *appellation contrôlée*. It was awarded by the English Vineyards Association.

Wines of the United States

Grapes are grown in 44 of the 50 United States. Without question, the two most important wine-making regions are California and the Finger Lakes area of New York State. Currently, the United States is ranked sixth in terms of the world's wine production.

American wines are labeled differently than European wines. The label may bear the name of the main grape variety used to make the wine, for example Cabernet Sauvignon or Chardonnay. These wines are known as *varietals*. Or, the label may have a name familiar to lovers of European wines, such as Chablis or Burgundy. These last two are called *generic* wines. The names suggest the kind of wine in the bottle. Usually, these cost less than varietal wines.

When discussing the flavors of American wines, it is important to distinguish wines made from native vine, such as *vitis labrusca*, and those made from European vines, such as *vitis vinifera*. California wines are made from grape vines brought from Europe long ago. Almost all other American wines are made from native varieties or hybrid vines bred from native vines.

California produces more than 85% of all American wine. Many are among the finest in the nation. New York State and other Eastern growing regions, such as the Lake Erie region of northern Ohio, are chiefly renowned for their champagnes. The sparkle in the wine moderates the strong flavor of native-American *vitis labrusca* grapes.

Technology is one reason for the rapid progress of the American wine industry. Many universities have

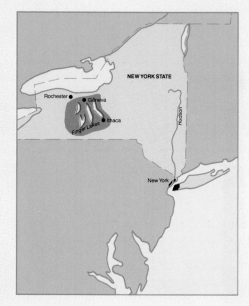

departments of viticulture (grape growing) and enology (wine making). Researchers develop wine-making techniques and cultivate new vine varieties suited to the different climates and soils found in American wine regions. Perhaps the most famous of these departments is at the University of California at Davis, which recently celebrated its 100-year anniversary.

California is blessed with many different types of climates and soils, so virtually every grape variety can be grown there. It is the task of the enologist to match grape and climate to make the best wine. Europeans have been doing this for centuries. Even so, there is always much more to learn.

Château St. Jean Gewürztraminer 1977;
Beaulieu Vineyard Pinot Noir 1977;
Gallo Hearty Burgundy;
Ridge Zinfandel 1976.

The future for American wines seems bright, thanks to a combination of ideal growing conditions, innovative wine makers, and a population that is learning more about wine.

OTHER WORDS USED WITH UNITED STATES WINES

American wine: US wine made outside of California.

Appetizer wine: Wine consumed before a meal to stimulate appetite. Also known as *apéritif* wine.

Barrel fermented: Fine wine fermented in oak casks.

Bottled by: The winery named on the label bottled wine produced elsewhere.

Brix: American wine makers measure the sugar content of grapes with a hydrometer. The scale of the hydrometer is read in Brix units. For example, 20° Brix means 20% sugar per 100g of grape juice. Some labels describe the sweetness of the wine grape this way.

Bulk process: A method used to make sparkling wines in large volume. The secondary fermentation occurs in a large tank instead of the bottle. Sediment is filtered instead of removed by hand. Also known as *Charmat* process.

Generic wine: Wine labeled with a borrowed European name. The wine is a typical example of a traditional wine, such as Chablis, claret, table wine, or vin rosé.

Jug wine: A wine (usually generic) sold in large containers at low prices.

Late-harvest wine: A sweet wine made from grapes picked with a high Brix or affected by *botrytis cinerea*.

Made and bottled by: This means that the winery named on the label produced at least 10% of the wine in the bottle.

Produced and bottled by: The named winery produced and bottled at least 75% of the wine in the bottle.

Varietal: Before 1983, this is a wine made from at least 51% of the grape variety named on the label. After January 1983, the percentage is 75%.

HISTORY OF AMERICAN WINE MAKING

Benjamin Franklin once said, "Wine is constant proof that God loves us and loves to see us happy." Therfore, it should be no surprise that wine-making in America is as old as the nation itself—and in some regions even older.

IN THE EAST

Wild grape vines existed in America before the earliest explorers. In addition, European colonists brought vines with them and attempted to make them flourish on the Eastern seaboard. Due to the relatively poor soil and climate, this experiment was not successful. Eventually, either by chance or design, some native-American grapes were crossbred with European grapes to create hybrid vines. These flourished, and many of today's Eastern wines are made with varieties descended from these vines.

IN THE WEST

Cortez, the Spanish conqueror of Mexico, ordered grapes to be planted in the New World during the late 16th century. These vines were brought from Europe.

In 1769, Father Junípero Serra, a Franciscan friar, established Mission San Diego and planted grapes there for making sacramental and medicinal wines. This *vitis vinifera* grape became known as the Mission grape. As the Franciscans moved north up the coast of what was to be California, they took cuttings from their vines and planted them at each new mission. Eventually, 29 missions were established from San Diego to Sonoma.

Commercial wine production began in 1824, when Joseph Chapman set up a winery in the Los Angeles area. Later, a Frenchman, Jean Louis Vignes imported vines from Europe to start a vineyard in Southern California. Until this time, most of the wines made in California had used the Mission grape. The quality of the wine was not very high.

Vignes realized that there was a demand for better wines. He began using choice grape types, such as the Cabernet Sauvignon. During the

1830s, hundreds of vine cuttings were sent on the long journey from France to Boston and then via Cape Horn to California.

The success of this venture meant a boom in the wine industry. Many Europeans who came to California during the gold rush stayed to grow grapes and make wine. Among these was a man named Count Agoston Haraszthy. This Hungarian had already made and lost several fortunes in the United States before settling in San Diego in 1849.

In 1857 he planted a vineyard in Sonoma, north of San Francisco. This area proved ideal for growing grapes, but Haraszthy knew that he could make better wine with better grapes. He talked to the Governor of the California, John G. Downey, and convinced him that wine making had a brilliant future in Northern California.

The Governor was impressed and commissioned the Count to visit Europe and obtain vine cuttings. During the next year, Haraszthy selected about 300 varieties. He shipped 100,000 cuttings from Europe to Cali-

fornia. He conducted rigorous experiments in his Sonoma vineyards to test which types grew best in certain conditions.

THE VINE LOUSE

Just as wine making in California seemed set for a bright future, disaster struck. In 1874 a vineyard in Sonoma County was found dying from the ravages of the vine louse called *phylloxera*. As mentioned earlier, this pest had already attacked and destroyed vast areas of European vineyards. The louse probably reached California in a shipment of infected cuttings.

Ironically, native-American vines, such as the *labrusca* varieties grown on the East Coast, were immune to the bug. Hardy, native-American root stock was used to save the vineyards. Grape growers grafted healthy cuttings from diseased vines to the *labrusca* root stock. These developed into healthy specimens with resistance to the pest.

In California and Europe, grape growers slowly replaced their devastated vineyards with grafted stock.

Even today there is no known treatment for *phylloxera*. Grafting is necessary almost everywhere that vines are grown.

By the end of the 19th century, the American wine industry began to revive. Many famous California names were associated with the business, including Leland Stanford and George Hearst. In l887, the University of California began its research-and-development programs of grape growing and wine making.

Annual production increased from about 4 million gallons in 1869 to 28 million by 1900 to almost 60 million in 1911. California wines began winning international competitions. This progress was cut short by Prohibition, which came into force in 1919 and lasted for 14 years. Many wineries closed, but some stayed in business by making sacramental or medicinal wine.

Since the repeal of Prohibition in 1933, the industry has been on a slow road to recovery. The upsurge of interest in California wines coincided with massive new plantings in all wine regions of the state during the 1970s.

Fountaingrove Vineyard in Santa Rosa was established by a religious order in 1875. In 1953, it was turned into a cattle ranch.

Left: Count Agoston Haraszthy was one of the pioneers of the California wine industry. He founded the Buena Vista Winery in 1857.

Opposite Page: A Spanish family at their Napa Valley Vineyard, about 1880.

CALIFORNIA RED GRAPES & WINE

Red grapes are planted throughout California's grape-growing regions.

Alicante Bouschet—Home wine makers like this thick-skinned red grape. Only one winery offers it in a varietal wine. Usually, it is used in blending.

Barbera—Much of this Italian grape becomes jug wine. Some wineries owned by Italian families use the grape in a varietal wine that is similar to the Barbera wines of northern Italy.

Burgundy—You'll see this name on generic red wines of California. It describes a dry red wine, not a fruity French-style Burgundy. California Burgundies are relatively inexpensive, and many are of higher quality than a French *vin ordinaire*. They are not meant for keeping. Drink them young.

Many wineries are now replacing the name Burgundy with California Red Wine, reflecting new pride in the industry. Few California wine makers now think of their wines as imitations of European wines.

Cabernet Sauvignon—Some of California's finest red wines use this grape. As mentioned earlier, the grape is also grown in the Bordeaux region of France and becomes classic clarets.

The best areas for its cultivation in California include Napa and Sonoma. Wines made of the grape are flavorful and powerful. Experts say that the wine tastes of black currants and olives. Most wines made from the grape are aged in oak casks, so they taste astringent when young. However, the wine mellows wonderfully in about 10 years. The good reputation of the varietal wine means high prices, especially for a good vintage. Some wineries offer a good non-vintage Cabernet Sauvignon at lower prices.

Carignane—This grape is used for blending in jug wines. It is mainly grown in central California. It is sometimes sold as an inexpensive varietal.

Chianti—Some wines made by some California wine makers of Italian descent use this as a generic name. Unlike the popular Italian red wine, the jug wines called Chianti in California are heavy and coarse. Usually, this is due to producers blending in a high proportion of rough wines from the

CABERNET
SAUVIGNON

PINOT NOIR

second or third pressing of a batch of grapes.

Claret—Simple California jug wines used to be called clarets. Today, most producers call claret-style wines California Red Wine.

Gamay Beaujolais—The flavor of the wine made from this California grape is light and fruity, similar to a French Beaujolais. Some Gamay Beaujolais is used in California rosés.

Grenache—In California the grape is used for both jug and varietal rosés. The wine has a distinctive color with an orange tint. The flavor is soft and said to resemble strawberries.

Grignolino—A light, red varietal with a spicy flavor. It is not very common.

Merlot—Wines made with this grape are softer and easier to drink young than varietal Cabernet Sauvignons. An increasing number of wineries are offering a Merlot varietal wine, but many use it to blend with Cabernet Sauvignon to give a fruity red wine.

Petite Sirah—There is much learned argument about the origins of this grape, but most growers believe it is related to the Syrah grape grown in the Rhône Valley of France.

Wines made with the grape have a pungent "black-pepper" aroma. Available as a varietal, it is sometimes used to add flavor to a blended wine.

Pinot Noir—Many enthusiastic wine makers are trying to improve the flavor of wines made with Pinot Noir, in spite of its reputation for failure in California. It is usually paler than a Cabernet Sauvignon and has a subtler taste. Be sure to ask your wine dealer for recommendations when purchasing this wine.

Ruby Cabernet—Researchers at the University of California at Davis developed this grape. They crossed the Carignane with Cabernet Sauvignon. The aim was to create a grape that had the best characteristics of both parents —a large harvest and good flavor respectively. It thrives in the hot regions of California and produces pleasant, soft wines of both jug and generic quality.

Zinfandel—For many wine drinkers, this grape is the essence of California. It can be made into a variety of wines, ranging from light rosé to a sweet, late-harvest red. There are some ordinary jug wines and many excellent varietal bottlings. The flavor is usually described as "berrylike."

As mentioned, Davis researchers have discovered that it came to California from Italy, solving a long unresolved mystery about its origin.

GAMAY

ZINFANDEL

These California wine labels show how the names of the grape is used on the label of a varietal.

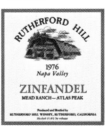

RUTHERFORD HILL
1976
Napa Valley
ZINFANDEL
MEAD RANCH — ATLAS PEAK
Produced and Bottled by
RUTHERFORD HILL WINERY, RUTHERFORD, CALIFORNIA
Alcohol 13.4% by volume

FREEMARK ABBEY
1976
NAPA VALLEY
CABERNET
SAUVIGNON
Produced and Bottled by
FREEMARK ABBEY WINERY, ST. HELENA, CALIFORNIA
Alcohol 13.5% by volume

Napa Valley wineries are known for their beautiful architecture. This is the Rhine House at the Beringer winery. It is a copy of the Rhine House in Mainz, Germany.

CALIFORNIA WHITE GRAPES & WINE

The white grapes of California that make the best wine seem to do best in the cool parts of the state. These include coastal valleys near the San Francisco Bay.

Chablis—You'll see this generic name on everyday white jug wine. In California the term usually denotes a light, blended jug wine made from such grapes as Chenin Blanc, French Colombard and Sauvignon Blanc. Some wineries bottle a high-quality Chablis that they say resembles those of France.

Chardonnay—Many connoisseurs claim that this grape produces California's most successful white wines. At its finest, varietal Chardonnay is fragrant and memorable. Unfortunately this acclaim has led to high prices and to some poor wines selling on the strength of the name alone. Chardonnay is sometimes aged in oak barrels, a rare practice with white wines.

Chenin Blanc—A widely available white jug and varietal wine. It is fruity and medium-sweet, so many inexperienced wine drinkers find it delightful. The best come from Napa and Sonoma, but some central California wineries produce good moderately priced Chenin Blancs.

Emerald Riesling—Like Ruby Cabernet, this is a successful crossbreed developed by the University of California at Davis. Wines made from it are often sweet, light and easy to drink. Hot regions of central California prove fatal to the flavor of many white grapes, but Emerald Riesling thrives there.

French Colombard—This grape produces fruity wines often used for blending because they are relatively high in acidity. It is the most commonly planted white variety in the state because it yields a prolific crop. It does well in hot areas but is also grown in Napa and Sonoma.

Fumé Blanc—Sauvignon Blanc grapes yield this crisp, dry white wine. The name was first used in the late 1960s when market research showed that American consumers had difficulty in pronouncing the name of the grape.

Gewurztraminer—This grape is well known in Germany, Austria and the Alsace region of France for producing spicy, fragrant wine in a range of

CHARDONNAY

CHENIN BLANC

wines from very dry to sweet. The same variety is available from California.

Grey Riesling—Do not confuse this grape with the Riesling of Germany. They aren't related. Most wines with this label are medium-sweet or "not quite dry." They are good wines with meals and are reasonably priced.

Johannisberg Riesling—The classic white grape of Germany makes good California wines. They have a distinctive style and "flowery" flavor that seem most attractive when made in a slightly sweet style. There are also some very sweet late-harvest styles similar to the *Auslese* wines of Germany. Because this grape is relatively difficult to grow, prices are high.

Malvasia Bianca—A fragrant, sweet white wine made from grapes grown in hot central California.

Moscato—Californians use the name for the muscat grape. It is used by several wineries for sweet wines. In this case, another name is usually added to the wine, such as Moscato Amabile and Moscato Canelli.

Muscat Blanc—The French use this name for the muscat grape. Wines called Muscat Blanc are usually sweet, spicy and fragrant.

Pinot Blanc—Even though this wine is less expensive than a Chardonnay, it has some of its characteristics. Generally, the Pinot Blanc is less pungent.

Rhine—Wine makers use the generic

name for a sweet, white wine.

Riesling—Any wine containing a variety of Riesling grape can be called Riesling. This makes it less expensive than Johannisberg Riesling. Many Riesling wines contain a high proportion of Grey Riesling and are made medium-sweet.

Sauterne—Sweet jug wines are generically named Sauternes, although dry Sauterne also exists. To be sure of what you are getting, read the label carefully.

Sauvignon Blanc—This popular dry white wine has a distinctive flavor of green pepper. In California it can also be known as Fumé Blanc. It is ideal as an apéritif or with food. Like Chardonnay, the best Sauvignon Blanc is aged in oak barrels.

Semillon—Together with Sauvignon Blanc, the Semillon is used in fine French Sauternes. In California it is used to make a variety of wines from dry to sweet, including jug wines.

Sylvaner—In California, the Sylvaner grape is mainly used for blending. It ripens early and has a flowery flavor like a Riesling. Some varietals are available.

Thompson Seedless—Only one winery offers this grape as a varietal wine and that is actually intended as a joke. This grape is mostly used as a table grape or dried to make raisins. In wine making, its blandness is good for blended jug wines.

RIESLING

SAUVIGNON BLANC

These are two labels from California white wines.

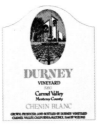

These are old vines in the winter, silhouetted against bare mountains. Inset: Grapes in flower before fruiting.

CHAMPAGNE & EASTERN VARIETIES

In the United States, domestic sparkling wines with bubbles due to a natural secondary fermentation may be called *champagne*. In the rest of the world champagne is a particular style of sparkling wine from the Champagne region of France, as described earlier. Any American wine that has been artificially carbonated, such as by adding soda water or carbon dioxide, is not called *champagne*.

Three methods are used in the United States to make champagne. The first is the French *méthode champenoise*, a costly process described earlier. The finest California wineries do this and charge high prices for their products.

The process may be hastened by transferring the wine from the bottle to a vat after the secondary fermentation. The sediment is filtered and the champagne rebottled and corked. This is the *transfer process*. It yields less expensive sparkling wines than those made with the *méthode champenoise*.

The third way is to use the *bulk*, or *Charmat*, process. In this method the secondary fermentation occurs in a large vat instead of in bottles. After this, the liquid is filtered and bottled. The quality of these sparkling wines is variable. Much depends on the quality of the grapes used.

CHAMPAGNE GRAPES AND TYPES

Grapes used in making US champagnes include the classic varieties used in France—Chardonnay and Pinot Noir. In the east, hybrid grapes such as the Delaware are used.

Blanc de Noir—Red grapes, such as the Pinot Noir, go into this white champagne. Even though the grapes have dark red skins, the juice is white after the grapes are pressed.

Blanc de Blancs—Only white grapes go into this type of sparkling wine. Some people think it has a delicate flavor.

Sparkling Burgundy—As the name implies, this is an ordinary red wine that sparkles. It is a generic name with no legal meaning.

Cold Duck—This is a sparkling wine made by blending a still Burgundy with a sweet champagne.

NEW YORK RED GRAPES AND WINES

After California, New York State produces more wine than any other state in America. Most New York vineyards are near lakes or large rivers in the western part of the state. The large bodies of water can extend the growing season by moderating the cool evening temperatures of early spring and late autumn.

Grapes for wine have been grown in this region for over 150 years. Most of today's grapes are descendants of native-American grape varieties.

Baco Noir—Flavorful, dark red wines are made with the grape. The hybrid is from a native strain called *vitis riparia*.

Catawba—Sweet red and rosé wines are made with the Catawba grape. It is from the *labrusca* family and has the characteristic pungent flavor of a wild grape. This flavor is also called "foxy."

Chelois—This French hybrid grape makes dry red wines. The taste is described as "slightly foxy."

Concord—Due to its fragrance and strong flavor, this grape is also used for grape juice and jellies. When used in wine, sugar is always added. Most kosher wines are made with Concord grapes.

De Chaunac—This variety is used to make dry red wines.

CATAWBA

SEYVAL BLANC

Above: This is the inside of a modern winery. Large fermentation vats are in a row. On the opposite side is a centrifuge for clearing sediment.

Left: Fine red wine is aged in barrels like these before being bottled.

NEW YORK WHITE GRAPES AND WINES

Aurora—You can get champagnes and light white wines made with the Aurora grape.

Delaware—This is another grape mainly used for champagne production. As a dry white wine it is pleasant and not excessively fragrant.

Dutchess—Semisweet wines are usually made with the grape.

Niagara—Wines made from it are either medium-dry or sweet, with a strong "foxy" flavor.

Scuppernong—The native grape has an unusual perfume-like aroma. It is made into sweet wines.

Seyval Blanc—Researches bred this vine to withstand cold climates. Wines made from it are usually dry and fruity.

Vidal Blanc—This is another French hybrid that makes fruity wines that can range from semisweet to dry.

NAPA VALLEY

Napa means *abundance* in the language of the early Indian inhabitants of this lovely area of California. The name is still richly deserved. Fertile vineyards spread across the valley floor and up steep slopes to higher sites where some of California's finest grapes are grown. The wineries here are pleasant and friendly places to vist. You can tour the facilities and taste their production.

A wide range of grape types are planted here because the valley's climate varies dramatically from south to north. To the south is the Carneros region not far from the San Francisco Bay. Wine makers here have to deal with cool breezes and mist in the evening and early morning.

Moving north, you'll find that the central part of the valley enjoys a temperate climate ideal for ripening most varieties of grapes. At the most northern part of the valley, near the old spa town of Calistoga, the climate is warmer.

However, not every winery makes wine only from grapes planted in nearby vineyards. Many bring in grapes from all over the valley, depending on the quality and success of the harvest that year.

State legislation is being introduced to make Napa Valley a region of defined quality, like the *appellation contrôlée* areas of France. Wines labeled *Napa* will have to be made with grapes grown within a certain area. This practically guarantees that Napa Valley wines will never be cheap.

Those from the tiny wineries now rival the best wines of Europe. And, those from large wineries often give outstanding value for the price.

The Beaulieu Vineyard—Frenchman Georges de Latour founded the winery in 1900. After his death, the family continued to run the business. They sold it in 1969. Its finest wines are made from Cabernet Sauvignon and labeled Georges de Latour Private Reserve.

Beringer Winery—In 1876, German brothers Jacob and Frederick Beringer founded this winery. Notable Beringer wines include Johannisberg Riesling and Pinot Noir, Chardonnay, and Fumé Blanc varietals. The winery also produces excellent red and white jug wines under the Los Hermanos label.

Carneros Creek—Fine Chardonnay, Pinot Noir and Zinfandel wines are made at this small winery. It is in the cool Carneros area, south of Napa.

Château Montelena—The original winery is over 100 years old. It produces some fine Chardonnay, Cabernet Sauvignon and Zinfandel wines.

The Christian Brothers—An order of teaching monks operates this winery to finance their schools. It is the largest Napa winery and has been here since 1930. Christian Brothers wines are sold all over the world. They are known for non-vintage, blended wines of all types that are made to be consumed young. They also make a popular dessert wine called Château La Salle.

Heitz Cellars Cabernet Sauvignon 1973;
Robert Mondavi Fumé Blanc 1978;
Domaine Chandon, Brut.

Clos Du Val—This winery is owned by Bernard Portet, who is related to some of the most talented wine-making families in the Bordeaux region of France. He makes fine red wines, featuring Zinfandel and Cabernet Sauvignon grapes. These wines age well.

Domaine Chandon—This winery is part of the Moët & Chandon company, makers of fine French champagne. Even though this winery uses the *méthode champenoise* to make their California champagne, the wine makers consider it sparkling wine.

Freemark Abbey—The old facilities of this winery were restored in 1965 by seven new owners. Their first wine was introduced in 1970, and since then they have gained a reputation for quality. Their most notable wines are Cabernet Sauvignon, Pinot Chardonnay and a special late-harvest sweet wine named Edelwein made from Johannisberg Reisling.

Heitz Cellars—Some of the Cabernet Sauvignon wines made by Joe Heitz are now legendary, commanding fabulous prices. He makes a variety of styles of wines, with ratings from good to superb. Perhaps the best indicator of this winery's quality is the fact that it is difficult to find these wines outside of California.

Inglenook—Like Beringer, this winery was founded in the late 19th century. It was family-owned and operated until 1964, when it was sold to a large company. It produces red and white wines of four categories. You can get vintage-dated, estate-bottled wine, single-vintage blends, and generic and jug wines.

Charles Krug Winery—This winery is owned by the Mondavi family. They produce a full range of red and wine varietal wines made of 100% of the grape name on the label. The jug wines are marketed under the name CK Mondavi.

Louis M. Martini—Good-quality inexpensive varietal wines are made at this family winery. White wines are made dry, and red wines are blends with names like Cabernet Sauvignon, Pinot Noir, Zinfandel. The generic wines are good values.

Robert Mondavi Winery—Robert Mondavi left the Charles Krug Winery to start this company in 1966. The company is progressive and modern. This winery was the first to introduce Fumé Blanc. Other notable wines are varietal wines, such as Cabernet Sauvignon, Chardonnay and Zinfandel.

Schramsberg Vineyards—The only product made here is champagne. Owner Jack Davies uses the traditional French methods from grape selection to *dosage* pioneered by champagne houses in Reims and Epernay. Output is relatively small and demand high.

Sterling Vineyards—The products of this beautiful winery have limited distribution. The best way to obtain these wines is to visit the facilities and taste them for yourself. They include red and white wines in both blends and 100% varietals.

SONOMA & MENDOCINO

Sonoma is west of the Napa Valley, closer to the Pacific Ocean. It has a moderate, well-balanced climate that is good for growing fine grape varieties. Many Sonoma vineyards are in the Russian River valley. There is a strong Italian influence here, as evidenced by such wineries as Italian Swiss Colony, Sebastiani, and Foppiano.

Like Napa, this region is the focus for an expanding wine industry. Wineries are being built and expanded, and new plantings continue. The Alexander Valley by the Russian River already has a reputation for good varietal wines even though the first vine was planted here about 1965.

Mendocino County north of Sonoma is another expanding area. The climate is a bit cooler, and the wines reflect the difference.

SONOMA

Buena Vista—Today the old stone buildings look much the same as they did in 1857, thanks to an extensive restoration program begun in 1943. The winery's most renowned wine is Zinfandel, but it makes a full range of varietals and fortified wines.

Italian Swiss Colony Vin Rosé;
Château St. Jean Chardonnay 1979;
Parducci Petite Sirah 1975.

Château St. Jean—The German wine maker here is well known for his German-style wines, such as Johannisberg Riesling and sweet late-harvest wines.

Hanzell Vineyards—Ambassador and financier James D. Zellerbach created this winery in Sonoma to make Burgundy-style Chardonnays and Pinot Noirs. Even the winery buildings are copies of the Clos de Vougeot in France. Zellerbach succeeded in making French-style wines until his death in 1963. Today the winery continues to make small amounts of superb wines.

Kenwood Vineyards—A group of young wine enthusiasts owns this winery. Its wines are mainly varietal. The best are the Cabernet Sauvignon, Zinfandel, Chenin Blanc and Johannisberg Riesling.

Sebastiani Vineyards—The largest wine producer in the Sonoma region, this family business has a mixture of old and new facilities, all located near the town of Sonoma. Its tour shows the scope of the business, which includes making a full selection of varietal, jug and fortified wines. Barbera is considered the best of its red wines. It is made with a traditional Italian grape type. Sebastiani also makes a young, fresh Gamay Beaujolais.

Dry Creek Vineyards—New Englander David Stare founded this winery in 1972. His venture is now a great success, with most critical praise going to his Fumé Blanc, Chenin Blanc and Chardonnay varietals.

Foppiano Wine Company—This Italian-family business was established in the final decade of the 19th century. The winery began as a producer of

good jug wines, but diversified into finer varietals. It now includes a full range of wines named after well-known grapes.

Geyser Peak Winery—Expansion of this winery has led to a larger variety of wines. They are produced under two labels—Voltaire and Summit. Voltaire wines are non-vintage varietals. They include Chenin Blanc, Pinot Chardonnay, Pinot Noir, Zinfandel and others. The Summit line includes good generic wines sold in bottles and jugs. Some are Napa Gamay, White Riesling, Rosé, Chablis, and Burgundy.

Italian Swiss Colony—Once a small, 19th century winery owned by one man, this large winery now produces a wide variety of wines under various labels, including fruit, appetizer and dessert wines. Some good wines under the Italian Swiss Colony label include some generic wines and non-vintage Cabernet Sauvignon and Zinfandel varietals.

Korbel—This winery is known for fine champagne made by the *méthode champenoise*. It also produces varietal and generic wines in addition to brandy.

Pedroncelli Winery—This is another Italian-family business with an inexpensive range of wines. These include some good jug wines and many varietals.

Sonoma Vineyards—Plantings in the 1970s give this winery a good list of vintage varietals. Some are Gamay Beaujolais, Zinfandel, Chardonnay, Cabernet Sauvignon, and Johannisberg Riesling.

MENDOCINO

Fetzer Vineyards—The Redwood Valley winery was founded in 1968. Its wines include generically labelled Mendocino Red and Mendocino White table wines, as well as a full list of varietals.

Parducci Wine Cellars—George and John Parducci offer a selection of varietal wines including Cabernet Sauvignon, Petite Sirah and Zinfandel red wines. The Sylvaner and Chardonnays are good white varietals.

Weibel Vineyards—Well known for sparkling wines, this Mendocino winery also specializes in making varietal wines and a range of table wines. Premium varietals include, Johannisberg Riesling, Chenin Blanc, and Pinot Noir.

MONTEREY & SANTA CLARA

If you travel south from San Francisco, you'll reach another vineyard region, not far from the factories and computer companies in so-called Silicon Valley. This area is really called Santa Clara Valley. It is fertile and warm and was once full of orchards. Today, wine making thrives here.

Rising above the Santa Clara Valley are the peaks of the Santa Cruz Mountains. Among the live oaks and redwoods of these lovely hills are a profusion of small wineries. Many specialize in making one or two varietal wines.

Farther south is the Gavilan mountain range in San Benito County. Like Santa Cruz, this region is alive with small, but good, wineries. The hills have outcrops of limestone soil, considered one of the finest soils for grapes. One such outcrop is at the Chalone Vineyard, which is producing Chardonnay and Pinot Noir in the best traditions of France.

The picturesque Monterey peninsula is cooled by ocean breezes. Around the inland towns of Salinas and Soledad are some grape-growing areas considered by experts to be the source of future fine wines. Many large wineries, including Almadén and Paul Masson, use grapes from the Monterey plantings for their varietal wines. Because the vines are still young, the flavor of the wine is sometimes "green" and too acidic. Innovative blending solves this problem. There is no doubt that the wines will improve as the vineyards mature.

Paul Masson California Red Wine;
The Firestone Vineyard Chardonnay 1979;
Ridge Zinfandel 1978;
Chalone Vineyard Pinot Blanc 1978.

SANTA CLARA AND SANTA CRUZ

Almadén Vineyards—Started in 1852 by two Frenchmen, Etienne Thée and Charles Lefranc, this large winery is now owned by a big corporation. It is one of the leading producers of California wine, with an annual volume over 15 million gallons. The Almadén wine list is extensive and includes several highly successful jug wines and more expensive varietals and sparkling wines. Mountain White and Mountain Red jug wines are good values.

Calera—Some vineyards are in limestone soil, like those of Chalone. Therefore, fine Pinot Noir is made in small quantities.

Chalone—The county's oldest winery is perched in solitary splendor above Monterey. It makes some exceptionally fine wines. Its Chardonnay, Pinot Blanc and Pinot Noir fetch high prices, but are well worth trying if you want to experience how good a California wine can be. Some of the vineyards are on limestone soil, like some of the best French vineyards.

David Bruce—This doctor-turned-winemaker makes small quantities of exceptional wines. Some experts say they have too much alcohol, but demand still exceeds supply. Look for full-bodied red wines such as Zinfandel, Pinot Noir and Petite Sirah.

Emilio Guglielmo—Thanks to a concealed cellar, the winery made wine during Prohibition. Its products are unpretentious and powerfully flavored. The Zinfandel is the winery's best-known product.

Jekel Vineyards—A range of varietals are made by the family-owned business. Some of the best are Chardonnay, Chenin Blanc and Cabernet Sauvignon made from grapes grown at surrounding vineyards.

Mirassou—The current owners of this winery are members of the fifth generation of American Mirassous. Their standards are high, and they make interesting powerful wines, such as Zinfandel, Chardonnay and Mirassou Cabernet. Both red and white varietals are aged in oak casks. Champagne is made here with the *méthode champenoise*.

Monterey Vineyards—Wines produced here are sold under the vineyard's label and also under the Taylor California Cellars label. Its white varietals are particularly interesting. Some excellent ones include Grüner Sylvaner, Chardonnay and Chenin Blanc. The only red wine made here is a Gamay Beaujolais.

Paul Masson—Even though this winery is owned by the world's largest liquor company, its wines are not just large production blends. The selection of dessert, apéritifs, and red and white varietals includes several quality wines from Monterey vines. There are also some house names for varietal wines, such as Emerald Dry made from Emerald Riesling grapes. Some pleasant jug wines are available in attractive carafes. Its champagne is made by the transfer process.

Ridge Vineyards—A group of Stanford professors owns this winery, which sits spectacularly atop a peak in the Santa Cruz Mountains. It is chiefly known for its full-bodied Zinfandel.

San Martin—Fruit wines, jug, and varietal wines are produced here. It also has a selection of vintage and non-vintage varietals, including Chenin Blanc, Johannisberg Riesling, Cabernet Ruby, and Petite Sirah.

SANTA YNEZ

The region surrounding the towns of Santa Ynez and Solvang, not far from scenic Santa Barbara, is one of California's most recent additions to the wine industry. Production is very small, but of high quality. Wineries include Firestone, Sanford & Benedict and Zaca Mesa.

CENTRAL CALIFORNIA

Unlike the pretty vine-covered slopes of Napa or Santa Clara, central California has a virtual sea of vines stretching for miles. The soil here is rich and fertile. All types of fruit and vegetables grow here, such as peaches, tomatoes and olives.

Because the temperature is very high all year, over-ripening is a problem for the grape grower. He must pick his grapes before they become too ripe or begin turning to raisins. Over-ripening can lead to a loss of subtle flavor, making the grapes mostly suitable for dessert wines and brandy.

Today, several factors are making central California wines better and better. One is the use of new grape varieties, such as the Emerald Riesling. It yields good-flavored grapes in a hot climate. Another is blending central California wines or grapes with others brought in from cooler areas like Napa or Sonoma. Many well-known wineries from other regions produce much of their wines from a mixture of grapes grown here.

Most of the production here is in the form of jug wines. Firms like Gallo and Franzia are enormous wine producers with giant wineries resembling oil refineries. These large wineries produce some very pleasant varietals too. They use the very latest wine-making techniques involving careful temperature control to keep the maximum flavor and freshness in the wine. Because production is large, prices are relatively low.

Farther north is one more California wine area. This is the historic gold country near the state capital, Sacramento. The climate is relatively cool for central California. Many small wineries are now in business.

Angelo Papagni—The specialty from this winery are vintage-dated varietals. It is the only winery to offer a varietal made from Alicante Bourschet. Its Chenin Blanc and Moscato are considered good white wines.

California Growers—This company has several labels for its wines, including Growers, Setrakian (well known for brandy) and LeBlanc. All are considered reliable wines with ordinary flavor.

Callaway Vineyards—It is in another new California wine area named Rancho California, in Riverside County. Its white wines have been especially successful, notably the Sauvignon Blanc.

Cribari—The wines made here are typical of this region. The best from this winery are the sweet dessert wines.

Delicato Vineyards—The family winery produces table and dessert wines for everyday consumption. The family name is actually Indelicato, but for obvious reasons the name of the winery is slightly different.

E & J Gallo—The remarkable achievement of Ernest and Julio Gallo has been to create the world's largest wine company. It is tucked away from the public gaze in unexciting Modesto. The different fruit and grape wines made under Gallo supervision represent one-third of California's wine production. The company is known for being secretive and does not allow tours of the winery.

Wines under the Gallo label are good jug and everyday wines. These include Hearty Burgundy and Chablis Blanc. The company offers a selection of varietals, such as Sauvignon Blanc, Zinfandel, and Ruby Cabernet, at very reasonable prices that make these high-quality *vin ordinaires*.

Greystone Malvasia Bianca;
Delicato Petite Sirah 1979;
Carlo Rossi Chablis.

Franzia—Like other central California wineries, it offers a selection of generic, appetizer and dessert wines. It recently introduced some varietals.

Giumarra—Varietal wines are produced here from grapes grown farther south, near Bakersfield. Red wines include Cabernet Sauvignon. Some white varietals are French Colombard and Chenin Blanc.

Guasti—Wines using this label name are made by the large California Wine Association. Other labels from the association include Ambassador and Greystone. Their wines include some well-made varietals and typical white and red jug wines. Brandy is also made.

Lamont—A grower's cooperative produces wines under this label. This is an unusual practice for California, but common in Europe. It produces a range of low-priced table wines.

Montevina—This winery is typical of those in the picturesque region near Sacramento. The steep foothill slopes of the Sierra Nevada mountains have a cool climate early in the year. Later the weather turns very hot. This is considered ideal for Zinfandel grapes. The best Zinfandel wines are eagerly sought by wine connoisseurs.

Perelli-Minetti—A range of vintage varietals are made here, including some white wines produced from Monterey grapes.

Petri—Most wine tasters say that the table and dessert wines made here are too sweet. This is called a "Valley" characteristic. It is a caramel-like taste due to over-ripening of the grapes.

NEW YORK STATE

Although New York is not the only state other than California to grow grapes and make wine, it has the largest production in the East. Other notable wine-making states include Ohio, Michigan, Virginia and Texas. However, none of these states make wines as good as those of the Finger Lakes region of western New York and the Hudson River Valley north of New York City.

These areas are probably best known to the consumer as growers of grapes that become New York Champagne. Many experts agree that the native and hybrid grapes grown here are best used in sparkling wines. Both table wines and champagne are sweet and taste of the "foxy" *labrusca* grapes. Even so, the large sales of New York wines such as Great Western Champagne indicate that many drinkers enjoy these products regardless of what many experts think about the superiority of European grapes.

Some wineries are introducing European grapes, such as Chardonnay, to the region. Wine makers like Konstantin Frank are making small amounts of table wine with grapes that ripen early. Connoisseurs agree that the wines made from these innovations are surprisingly good.

These developments have not significantly affected the main output of New York wineries. Most production is sweet, generic wines with labels like Burgundy and Sauterne. The flavor

Benmarl Nouveau 1980;
Taylor Rhine Wine;
Gold Seal Catawba Pink;
Gold Seal Champagne.

depends on which strain of grapes is used to make the blend. Wines made with mostly native varieties have a stronger and "foxier" flavor. And, some New York wineries use California wine in some blended wines. Wines made with French-American hybrid grapes, like the Seyval Blanc, have a less pungent flavor and taste more like their European predecessors.

Benmarl—Like other Hudson Valley wineries, this one specializes in wines from French-American hybrids such as Seyval Blanc.

Brotherhood—A traditional winery making sweet table wines and fortified wines. It also has varietals, including Chelois.

Gold Seal—This is an old firm with a willingness to experiment. It was the first to produce a wine from European *vinifera* grapes. It now has both Riesling and Chardonnay vineyards. Also well known is their Blanc de Blancs champagne, named after their French champagne maker Charles Fournier.

Great Western—This is probably the best-known name on the New York wine scene. Besides sparkling wine, this company also makes varietal wines, including Seyval Blanc and Baco Noir.

Monarch—This company is based in Brooklyn and makes Manischewitz

kosher wines. These are very sweet.

Royal—This is another kosher winery in the Hudson Valley. Their product is sold under the Kedem label.

Taylor—Many Taylor wines are made with native grapes and tend to be "foxy." The company produces 62 wines, including appetizer, dessert, table and sparkling wines. It is the largest producer of New York wines, with a capacity of about 24 million gallons.

Vinifera Wine Cellars—Konstantin Frank, who first worked for Gold Seal, owns this winery. He offers varietals made from European grapes, including Chardonnay, Riesling and Muscat Ottonel.

Widmer—This old firm produces a full range of wines from both native grapes and hybrids. Their labels include Lake Niagara table wines and a varietal made from the Delaware grape.

Wines of Australia & New Zealand

Grape vines came to Australia in 1788 with the First Fleet of the British Navy. Captain Arthur Phillip planted the first vineyard. By 1820, wine was made in New South Wales on a large scale. By 1840, vineyards spread to Victoria, South Australia and Western Australia. Descendants of the first wine-making families still tend the best vineyards. The biggest wine-producing states are South Australia, New South Wales and Victoria. Small amounts of wine are made in Queensland, Western Australia and the island of Tasmania.

Australia makes generic and varietal wines. Everyday table wines are called Chablis, Burgundy or Sauterne, indicating their general style and sweetness. Varietal wines have the name of the grape type, such as Riesling or Shiraz.

There are also fine, estate-bottled wines that name the vineyard, proprietor, and vintage, such as Tollana 1980 Rhine Riesling or Wynns Coonawarra Estate Hermitage 1976. A good way to choose an Australian wine is to pick a favorite grape variety, good vintage and grower. Your wine dealer can help you do this.

RED GRAPE VARIETIES

Because the climate in the coolest parts of Australia resembles that of the hottest parts of Europe, it is difficult to make delicate red wines. Traditional Australian red wines are sweet because they are made from very ripe grapes.

Cabernet Sauvignon—In Australia this grape makes a rich, full-bodied wine benefiting from several years of storage before being consumed.

Shiraz—The Syrah of the French Rhône Valley and the Petite Sirah of California are related to the Shiraz. It flourishes in hot climates and is used in both generic and varietal wine of all price categories. At its best, it rivals Cabernet as a grape for top-quality red

Tolland Rhine Riesling;
Saltram Rhine Riesling 1980;
Yalumba Rossa Cabernet Sauvignon 1975;
Hardy's Nottage Hill Shiraz.

wines. Sometimes the two varieties are blended. This grape is also called Hermitage.

Grenache—In Australia, this grape is used to make a light, fresh rosé.

WHITE GRAPE VARIETIES

Australian tastes for white wines are changing due to the popularity of fruity German wines. New techniques of cold fermentation in stainless steel vats mean that more flavor can be extracted from the grapes and alcoholic content controlled to "German" strength. The result is a range of delightful dry or medium-dry white wines.

Rhine Riesling—This makes good dry white wines with plenty of flavor and acidity.

Semillon—Australian wine makers use the grape to make dry white wines benefiting from wood aging.

Traminer—German-style wines are made with blends of Traminer and Riesling.

Verdelho—This Portuguese variety yields soft wines with a fragrant bouquet.

Muscat Blanc—Rich, sweet wines with a full grape flavor are made with this grape.

Ugni Blanc—Fruity dry wine is made from Ugni Blanc, also known as the White Shiraz.

NEW SOUTH WALES

Australian wine-making began in this area. The best area is the Hunter River Valley where the soil is volcanic. Red wines are made chiefly of Shiraz and blended with some Cabernet Sauvignon.

Two area names to look for on wine labels are Pokolbin and Rothbury. Estates include Lindeman's Ben Ean, Lake's Folly, The Rothbury Estate, Drayton's Bellevue and Penfold's Dalwood.

Another good wine area is Mudgee, on higher ground than the Hunter Valley, but yielding similar styles of dry red and white wine. The Riverina is a hot, flat area that produces ordinary table wines. Because of little rainfall here, new irrigation techniques have been developed to pipe water from the Murrumbidgee River. This has improved vineyards and allowed a larger variety of grapes to grow.

VICTORIA

About 15% of Australia's wine is made here. Vineyards in the Great Western area rise to a high of 1,000 feet, and the soil is rich in lime, making it ideal for grape-growing.

The major firms are Seppelt and Best. Seppelt's most widely distributed product is good sparkling wine. They also make a range of varietal red and white wines.

Glenrowan-Milawa—Some interesting white and red wines are made here, notably some long-lived Shiraz. Look for Booth and Brown Brothers.

Goulburn-Tabilk—Château Tahbilk, a red wine made with Cabernet and Shiraz, is the best wine from this small region north of Melbourne.

Mildura—Dessert wines and ordinary table wines, both red and white, are made here.

Rutherglen—Wineries on the hot plains of the Murray River make top-quality dessert wines and excellent full-bodied "old-style" red wines. These are high in alcohol and should be aged for several years before being consumed. Names to look for include Morris, Smith, Seppelt and Chambers.

SOUTH AUSTRALIA

Australia's most renowned wine region is the Barossa Valley. Fruity white wines made from the Rhine Riesling are especially well made. The region was originally settled by German immigrants and the wines reflect this.

Most major Australian wineries have vineyards here, including Seppelt, Lindeman, Penfold, Thomas Hardy, Henschke and Gramp. There is also a giant cooperative making good wines under the name Kaiser Stuhl.

Basedows Shiraz;
Quelltaler Riesling 1979;
Balgownie Cabernet Sauvignon 1976;
Tulloch Pokolbin Semillon 1978.

Good red wines from this area are made with blends of Cabernet Sauvignon and Shiraz. They are lighter in style than those of Victoria.

Coonawarra—The name means "wild honeysuckle" in the Aborigine language. This is a small area with a worldwide reputation for good wine. In the far southwest, the climate is relatively cool and grapes can ripen slowly. Producers include Wynns, Redman and Lindeman. The Wynns Coonawarra Estate Cabernet Sauvignon is outstanding.

Southern Vales—The climate in this area south of Adelaide is cool. Fine vineyards here include Hardy's Tintara and Kay Brothers' Amery.

QUEENSLAND

Fortified and dessert wines are produced in this hot, northern region.

WESTERN AUSTRALIA

Near Perth are two relatively new areas showing promise for the future. Swan Valley has some good Cabernet Sauvignon red wines. The Margaret River area is planted with a wide range of varieties.

TASMANIA

The climate of this island is a bit too cool and damp for fine grapes. However, experimental vineyards of Chardonnay, Traminer and Rhine Riesling are planted. They may yield some good wines in due course.

NEW ZEALAND

The climate here is near ideal for growing grapes. Most grapes are grown in the North Island near Auckland and in the Hawke's Bay district, which is relatively drier. Varietals planted include Chardonnay, Cabernet Sauvignon and Pinot Noir. Some producers to look for include McWilliams, Cook's, and Montana.

Wines of South America

South America's two major wine producers are Argentina and Chile. Wine experts agree that the red Cabernet from Chile is very good and could compete with the best of Europe or the United States.

Chile has vineyards that were never affected by the vine louse *phylloxera*, which virtually wiped out the vines of Europe and the United States. The central valleys of Chile have a temperate climate, ideal for grape growing. The Chilean government monitors wines for export. *Reservado* wines are at least four years old, and *gran vino* wines are at least six years old.

Argentina's wine production is fourth in the world, yet very little is exported. Wine is an everyday drink in Argentina, and internal demand keeps up with supply.

Most Argentinian wine is grown on the plateaus of Mendoza, in the shadow of the Andes. Argentinan vineyards have over 275 days of sun every year and plenty of water from melted snow from the Andes. Red and white wines are made from European grape varieties.

GRAPE VARIETIES

For full-bodied red wines of Argentina, the main grape varieties are the Cabernet Sauvignon, Malbec and Merlot. All were originally from the Bordeaux area of France. White wines are also made with varietals well known in France, including the Chardonnay and the Chenin Blanc.

In the 19th century the Chilean wine industry, which was started by Catholic missionaries, was assisted by wine makers from Bordeaux. They brought cuttings of Bordeaux grapes, including Cabernet and Merlot for red wines, and Sauvignon Blanc and Semillon for white wines.

ARGENTINA

The Mendoza plains of Argentina are hot, but the climate is slightly moderated by cool air from the Andes. As in all hot climates, modern technology and cool fermentation methods have improved the quality of the table wines made here.

Andean—Five major growers use this name for their well-made dry varietal wines, including Chenin Blanc, Chardonnay and Cabernet.

Angel Furlotti—This producer makes good white and red wines, including Cabernet and Riesling.

Pascual Toso—Cabernet, Riesling, and sparkling wines are made by this well-known producer.

CHILE

The main area for Chilean wine production is centered on the valleys of the Aconagua, Maipo and Cachapoal rivers. The soil here is light, but fertile.

Aconagua Valley—North of Valparaiso and Santiago in central Chile is the Aconagua Valley. Wineries here make some of the best Chilean Cabernet and Merlot wines.

Maipo Valley—South of Santiago is this valley known for several wineries, including Cousino-Macul. Cabernet made here is aged in oak casks from France. Wineries also offer a good dry Semillon, Chardonnay, and fine Cabernet.

Santa Ana—Undurraga is another name seen on bottles of exported Chilean wine. Wines made in this area west of Santiago are not as fine as those of Maipo, but generic Burgundy and varietal wines are good values.

Chilean Gran Vino Cabernet, Conch y Toro, Maipo 1973;
Argentine Red Wine, Mendoza;
Chilean Cabernet Sauvignon, Viña Linderos, Maipo 1978.

Wines of South Africa

The first vineyards in South Africa were established by Dutch settlers in the 17th century. Wine has been made ever since. The climate resembles that of the Australian wine-making regions. In fact, South African wine makers have similar problems with overripe grapes. As a result, South African sherry and other fortified and dessert wines are generally better known than the table wines.

GRAPE VARIETIES

The two major wine towns of South Africa are Paarl and Stellenbosch. Paarl makes a good Spanish-style sherry. Stellenbosch produces very fine estate-bottled wines. Both areas make ordinary table wines, too.

There is a system of *appellation contrôlée* for South African wines. The authenticity of the label is guaranteed by a seal on the neck of the bottle.

Paarl's climate is hot, dry and suited to the production of dessert wines. Grapes grown here include Muscadel, Muscat of Alexandria, and Palomino, the grape used for sherry.

Stellenbosch lies closer to the coast and the city of Cape Town. Cool breezes from the ocean help make the climate temperate. Conditions are suitable for the classic grape varieties. White grapes are grown on light, sandy soils. One highly successful grape grown here is the Steen, related to the Chenin Blanc of the Loire Valley. Semillon and Riesling are also grown and made into white table wines.

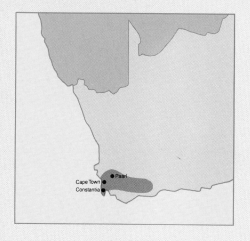

Full-bodied red wines are made from grapes grown in granitic soil. These grapes include Cabernet Sauvignon, Shiraz, and Pinotage, a cross between the Pinot Noir and the Cinsaut.

Theuniskraal Riesling, Tulbagh 1979;
Meerlust Cabernet Sauvignon, Stellenbosch 1975;
Pinotage, Groot Constantia, 1976;
KWV Roodeberg, Paarl 1976.

CONSTANTIA

Wine called Constantia was as famous as Hungarian Tokay or French Sauternes in the 19th century. It was a rich, sweet wine served to the crowned heads of Europe. Even today it commands high prices when it appears at special wine auctions.

The Groot Constantia estate on the coast near Cape Town makes many top quality varietal wines, including Cabernet and other strong red wines.

STELLENBOSCH

The town gives its name to the region. The most famous producer here is the Stellenbosch Farmers' Winery Cooperative. It produces excellent vintage white and red wines under a variety of labels and brand names, one of which is Meerlust.

PAARL

Even though this area is known for its sherries, many pleasant table wines are made here. A name to look for is Nederburg, which makes wines in all price categories from simple table wine to a rare sweet wine called Edel-keur. Their wines are seen by the world's wine importers at a special annual auction of South African wines, usually held in March.

The state cooperative, with the brand name KWV, makes a selection of good table wine with reasonable prices. The white Steen is crisp and dry. Pinotage is a dry, fruity red varietal.

TULBAGH

This important wine region is north of Paarl. One famous estate here is Twee Jongezellen, which includes Riesling and Steen among its best wines.

LITTLE KAROO

Ordinary table wine comes from this dry, hot district. Much is distilled into brandy, a favorite drink of South Africans.

Appetizer & Dessert Wines

You can enjoy many of the wines already mentioned as appetizer and dessert wines. Or, you can choose a fortified wine for pre- and post-dinner consumption. A fortified wine has more alcohol than a regular wine—typically 16 to 20% as compared with 10 to 14%.

The additional alcohol is due to the addition of a spirit, such as brandy, during fermentation. The high alcoholic content stops fermentation, leaving some sugar in the wine. This is why many fortified wines are sweet. A dry fortified wine is made by adding spirit after fermentation is complete.

APPETIZER WINES

By definition, an appetizer wine should stimulate your appetite before a meal. It should not fill you up or mask the flavors of the food and wine you will have with the meal. Generally, it should be cold, not too strong, and dry. A dry white wine or champagne are sometimes used. Here are some others.

Sherry—This drink is made in many countries of the world, but true sherry is made in Jerez, Spain. In 1967 a British court ruled that what is called sherry in Britain must be from Spain. Any other sherry-type drinks must be named with the country of origin, such as South African Sherry or Cyprus Sherry. In the United States, sherry is less popular, so there is less distinction made between US and Spanish sherries.

Spanish sherry is made by a particular method, which like champagne is often imitated but never duplicated. Wines destined to become sherry are stored in oak casks. As the wine ages, a white film of mold called *flor* forms on the surface of the wine. It alters the

Noilly Prat French Extra Dry Vermouth;
Martini Rosé;
Martini Rosso Vermouth;
Cinzano Bianco Vermouth;
Tio Pepe Dry Sherry;
Old Malmsey Madeira.

flavor and gives a distinctive taste. After a year the wine is lightly fortified with Spanish brandy—then aged in oak barrels for several more years before being bottled.

The barrels are stored in tiers, grouped in a special way to form a *solera*. The *solera* system of aging is important in the making of a true sherry. Wine is drawn off from the lower tiers and then some sherry from the upper tiers is added, making a continuous blend of old and new sherries. The name *solera* comes from the Spanish word for sun. Traditionally, the *solera* was out in the sunshine so the young sherry would evaporate and concentrate its flavors.

This method is now imitated by wine makers in other countries, including the United States. The Sebastiani winery in California's Sonoma Valley has its own solera.

After the sherry is aged and blended, it is ready for bottling. According to the level of sweetness required, special sweet wine is added. Some different sherries are:

Fino: Light and dry.
Amontillado: Medium dry.
Manzanilla: Very pale and dry.
Oloroso: Darker and heavier than Fino, medium-sweet.
Cream: Sweetened Oloroso. Also used as a dessert wine.

Madeira—The story of Madeira is a curious one. It is named after the island in the Atlantic where the fortified wine is still made. In the seafaring days of the British Empire, ships would stop at this Portuguese island to obtain barrels of wine for long voyages. The sailors would add brandy to the barrels so the wine would not spoil. During the journey, the wine heated up in the hold of the ship and prematurely aged. This improved the flavor.

The process was copied by the wine makers of Madeira when they realized how it improved their wines. Today, wine for Madeira is heated to about 120F (50C) for several months in an *estufa,* or hot house. Brandy is added, and the madeira is blended in the same way used for sherry. Some styles of madeira are:

Sercial: A light dry wine.
Verdelho: Medium-dry golden wine.
Bual: Medium-sweet wine.
Malmsey: Very sweet and rich.

Vermouth—The origins of vermouth are in herbal medicine, when wine was blended with herbs and aromatic extracts. The name Vermouth is derived from *wermut,* a German word for wormwood. Its bitter-tasting flowers are used in vermouth.

Today, vermouth is made by adding brandy to light wine, then flavoring it with a mixture of up to 50 herbs. Each vermouth manufacturer has his own special recipe.

Not long ago, a French vermouth was considered a dry white style. An Italian vermouth was a sweeter red blend. These countries now make both styles, in addition to medium-sweet *bianco* and a rosé vermouth. Other wine-making nations also produce vermouth.

DESSERT WINES

Most dessert wines are sweet. They can be consumed with fruit, cheese, a creamy dessert, or all by themselves. Generally, red dessert wines are best at room temperature. White and brown dessert wines are good when chilled.

Port—The British take credit for inventing this fortified wine. According to one story, Portuguese wine shipped to England spoiled during the voyage. One shipper added brandy to the wine in an attempt to preserve it. The result was a much-improved product.

It is a rich, full-bodied fortified wine made in red, white, and amber colors. True port from Oporto, Portugal is widely imitated but not yet duplicated. To make port, fermentation of the original wine is halted with brandy. Then the young port is aged in wooden casks for two or more years. This mellows the flavor of the wine. These "wood" ports are described on the label as *Ruby* or *Tawny.* Tawny port is older, browner, and less fruity than Ruby port. It is usually more expensive too.

The best port, called *Vintage,* is bottled after aging in a wooden cask for two years. Then it ages in the bottle for at least 10 years. Vintage port is made from the best grapes of good harvests. Famous brands of vintage port include Warre, Dow, Cockburn and Croft.

Some California wineries make excellent ports. The wine makers use the same grape varieties planted in the Douro region of Portugal. Some good brands of California port include Ficklin, Paul Masson, J.W. Morris and Woodbury. Other countries making pleasant port-style wines are Australia and South Africa.

Marsala—Sicily is the home of this sweet fortified wine. It is dark brown and has an alcoholic content between 18 and 20%. One grade of Marsala, *Speciali,* is flavored with egg, almonds, or strawberries.

Muscat Wines—The scented, fragrant muscat grape is made into dessert wines all over the world. Not all are fortified. Some have high alcoholic content because of the high sugar content in the ripe grapes.

In California and Australia, a wide range of Muscat dessert wines are made. These include dark Muscatel made from Black Muscat grapes, and golden Muscatels made with the Muscat of Alexandria grape.

Widmer Port;
Marsala all'uovo;
Muscat de Beaumes de Venise;
Cockburn's Special Reserve Port.

The fortified Muscat de Frontignan and Muscat de Beaumes de Venise made in the South of France are delicious with fruit.

Tokay—The original Tokay is a sweet wine from Hungary, never fortified. However, in California this name is used for a sweet, port-style drink made with a blend of California port, sherry and Angelica, a pale fortified wine made from white grapes.

Summer & Winter Wine Drinks

Some wines are good when mixed with ice and other fruits and liquids. This is a fine way to appreciate less-expensive table and jug wines. These recipes call for standard bottles of wine, about 25.5 fluid ounces.

COOL SUMMER DRINKS

SANGRIA

Use a full-bodied red wine and citrus juices to make this Spanish-style drink. Put the following ingredients in a punch bowl or large jug: a couple of trays of ice, juice from an orange and a lemon, two or three sliced oranges, and about a half cup of sugar to taste. Pour in a bottle of dry red Spanish wine, or the equivalent, such as California Burgundy or Zinfandel. Add a splash of soda water, if desired. Stir and serve.

SUMMER WINE CUP

Chill two bottles of German Hock or Mosel, or California Riesling or Rhine wine. Pour about three ounces of Curacao liqueur and three ounces of Maraschino liqueur into a punch bowl or large jug. Add a couple of trays of ice, pour in the wine and stir. Add soda water, if desired. Decorate each glass with cocktail cherries or fresh fruit in season.

MIMOSA

Mix equal amounts of well-chilled champagne or sparkling wine with fresh orange juice. Add one-half fluid ounce of brandy for every bottle of champagne used. Brandy is optional. No ice is necessary.

STRAWBERRY CHAMPAGNE PUNCH

Serve your guests this elegant punch at your next celebration. Cut six lemons and six oranges into thin slices. Marinate the slices in a punch bowl containing the contents of two bottles of sweet, non-fortified dessert wine and eight fluid ounces of brandy. A French Sauterne or California Malvasia is a good choice of wine. Let the mixture chill for at least 12 hours in the refrigerator.

When ready to serve, add two bottles of chilled champagne or sparkling wine to the bowl. Purée a pound of fresh or frozen strawberries in a blender. Stir them into the bowl. Decorate the top of the punch with fresh strawberries and mint leaves. You can also substitute apricots or peaches for strawberries.

CHAMPAGNE COCKTAIL

Put a sugar cube in the bottom of a wine glass. Add three dashes of Angostura Bitters. Add one-half fluid ounce of brandy. Top with cold champagne or sparkling wine and decorate with a slice of orange. This drink looks very attractive in a flat, dish-shaped champagne glass.

KIR

In Burgundy, this is a traditional appetizer. Pour four fluid ounces of chilled, dry white wine into a wine glass. Add a dash of Cassis, which is a black currant liqueur. Stir and serve.

WARM WINTER DRINKS

MULLED WINE

Hot, spicy wine is a welcome drink on a cold evening. First, you make a spicy syrup. Mix one teaspoon ground cloves, one teaspoon ground nutmeg, two teaspoons ground cinnamon, one-half of a diced orange, one-half of a diced lemon, five ounces of sugar, and 16 fluid ounces of water. Boil the mixture for one hour. Then strain it through a fine sieve or cloth.

Second, mix the syrup and a bottle of dry red wine in a pan. Heat the liquid, but do not boil. Serve in cups with cinnamon sticks and sliced citrus fruits.

HOT PUNCH

Cut 10 slices of lemon and put several cloves in each slice. Mix two bottles of medium-dry Madeira, 10 fluid ounces of brandy, one-half pound of sugar, and 10 cinnamon sticks in a pan. Heat this, while stirring constantly, to near boiling. Serve hot in cups with a lemon slice on top.

Strawberry Champagne Punch

Index

ACKNOWLEDGMENTS

I would like to thank the following individuals and organizations for their kind assistance in making this book:
Australian Wine Centre, London; Chinacraft Ltd., London; Nicholas Clarke, MW, Henry C. Collison & Sons Ltd, London; Aldwyn Cooper, Covent Garden General Store, London; Richard Dare Kitchen Utensils, London; Del Monico Wines Ltd., London; Julie Fitzherbert-Brockholes; German Food and Wine Centre, London; German Wine Information Service, London; Grierson-Blumenthal Ltd., London; Tony Laithwaite, Sunday Times Wine Club, London; Geoffrey Roberts Ltd., London; The Wine Institute, San Francisco; The Wine Society, London.

Picture Credits:
Anthony Blake, 11; Cooper Bridgeman, 8-9, 22-23; Werner Forman Archive, 10 (bottom left); Fotomas Index, 10 (top left); Peter Newark's Western Americana 78; John Topham, 6; John Yates, 81; California Wine Institute, 13, 79 (top and left), 83, 85 (top and bottom). All other photos by Peter Myers. Illustrations by Elaine Keenan. Maps and diagrams by Chris O'Connor.

2.8263012621